CROWNING GLORIES

Discover the Arrow Crown Block • 9 Quilt Projects
Over 80 Design Possibilities

Lerlene Nevaril

Text © 2005 Lerlene Nevaril
Artwork © 2005 C&T Publishing
Publisher: Amy Marson
Editorial Director: Gailen Runge
Acquisitions Editor: Jan Grigsby
Editor: Sarah Sacks Dunn
Technical Editors: Robyn Gronning, Gael Betts, René Steinpress and Sara MacFarland
Copyeditor/Proofreader: Wordfirm, Inc.
Cover Designer: Kristy K. Zacharias
Design Director/Book Designer: Kristy K. Zacharias
Illustrator: Richard Sheppard
Production Assistant: Tim Manibusan
Photography: Luke Mulks and Diane Pedersen unless otherwise noted
Published by C&T Publishing, Inc., P.O. Box 1456, Lafayette, CA, 94549
Front cover: *Indonesian Splendor*
Back cover: *Memories from the Mills, Autumn Richness*

Library of Congress Cataloging-in-Publication Data
Nevaril, Lerlene,
Crowning glories : discover the arrow crown block, 9 quilt projects, over 80 design possibilities / Lerlene Nevaril.
p. cm.
Includes bibliographical references.
ISBN 1-57120-282-X (paper trade)
1. Patchwork--Patterns. 2. Quilting--Patterns. I. Title.
TT835.N467 2005
746.46'041--dc22
2005016924

Printed in China

10 9 8 7 6 5 4 3 2 1

I dedicate this book to
Tomme Fent, who gave me the idea.

Acknowledgments

I want to thank everyone at C&T who made this second book as great an adventure as the first. They have taken my idea and made it bloom and blossom. I also want to thank the machine quilters who brought my quilt tops to life: Jan Korytkowski, Mary Roder, Wanda Jones, and Lyla Pack. I am in awe of their talents. And finally, my thanks to my family and friends for their support throughout the adventure.

Contents

Introduction

Artists often produce works in series: they develop a technique or special way of interpreting a single idea or image. Some quilters do the same. For example, Paula Nadelstern and Patricia Campbell keep amazing us with their variations and new ideas for kaleidoscopes and Jacobean appliqué. I once knew a man who celebrated the same age several birthdays in a row, because, he said, some ages are so good they can't be fully experienced in just 12 months.

What encourages this dedication to a single idea or design? It's the old "What if..." phenomenon. What if I change the color, the mood, the fabric, the paint, the line, etc? It's also the comfort level. Find something you like, keep repeating it—with variety—and it becomes second nature. The more you do something, the easier it gets. With enough innovation, an idea never comes out the same way twice. It's recognizable, like an old friend, but it's fresh and new each time.

When I began looking at quilt blocks, I saw that hidden inside complex blocks were simpler blocks just begging to be used. They worked well as companions to the original blocks because they had some of the same lines. When two or more of these blocks were combined, exciting new quilt designs emerged. My head began to reel with the possibilities. I ran to the computer and began to play. My first book, *Hidden Block Quilts,* was the result. In that book, I explored ten quilt blocks, and presented nine quilt designs using each. That was only scratching the surface on some of the blocks—I had so many ideas that it would take a lifetime to make them all.

The Arrow Crown is a block full of design possibilities. According to Barbara Brackman in her *Encyclopedia of Pieced Quilt Patterns,* the Arrow Crown is a four-patch block with 64 squares, credited to Thelma Heath, ca. 1940. Its many squares and triangles offer dozens of opportunities for numerous hidden blocks. It looks good set straight or on-point. It has no curves or set-in shapes. In short, it is an almost perfect block with which to play.

I did just that, and I found the 34 hidden blocks presented in this book. Statistically, I have almost 32,000 possible quilts from just these 35 blocks (including the original). That's almost three quilts per day for 30 years!

Come explore the Arrow Crown block with me. It will open your eyes to the exciting possibilities of working in series. Your life will never be the same—and neither will your quilts!

How to Use This Book

When I started working with hidden blocks, I was looking for alternate blocks that complemented the original block, yet had fewer pieces and were easier to construct. Once I realized I could abandon the original block altogether, I designed quilts that were lighter and more open. The first Arrow Crown hidden blocks all had a common trait: The outer row of patches was replaced by sashing strips (see the 8 × 8 grid blocks on page 7).

As I studied these designs, I had a "What if…" idea. What if I eliminated the outer row of patches entirely, and changed these to 6 × 6 grid blocks? A second set of blocks was born (see the 6 × 6 grid blocks on page 16).

Quilters find working with 2″ units very comfortable. But in an 8 × 8 (64-piece) block, the finished block would measure 16″. This makes quilts get very big, very fast. Quilts have a more pleasing composition if you use 12″ or smaller blocks, especially bed-size quilts. Wall quilts, on the other hand, have more movement if you use 9″ blocks.

As a result, the 8 × 8 grid blocks in this book measure 12″ finished, and the units 1½″. The 6 × 6 grid blocks measure 9″; these units are also 1½″. This is an easy size to work with, and the blocks "look good." While none of the designs in this book combines the two sets of blocks, the quilt police are not going to knock on your door if you want to experiment in that direction.

You'll find all the blocks used in the project quilts beginning on page 8. The project blocks have cutting and sewing directions for assembly. The quilt projects begin on page 27, and include a materials chart with the fabrics to use for each block referenced.

The blocks not used in the projects are used in the gallery quilts, and are presented in the Block Gallery on page 68. The project and gallery blocks used in each gallery quilt are listed with the quilt.

The uniqueness of each quilt design is the result of the blocks used and the distribution of color in the design. Color can be used to form secondary designs where the blocks meet (see pages 53–54). In the *Autumn Richness* quilt (page 32) brown corner squares add a Nine Patch illusion at the corners of the four center blocks. In the quilt *Pastel Dreams* (page 50), using both pink and cream backgrounds in the L and X blocks gives the illusion of a pink inner border. Notice how changing background colors adds extra interest to one of the gallery quilts on page 71.

The quilt designs are organized by quilt setting, size, and design. There are four horizontal settings and five on-point settings. Each quilt contains complete directions for cutting and assembly. As a bonus, there are 9 additional quilt designs included in a gallery after each quilt—these show different blocks (and colors) that you can substitute into each setting for different looks.

Make the quilts as shown, play with one of the gallery designs, or substitute gallery blocks that you like best. Trade border designs, add or take out sashings, and play with background colors. Once you decide on a design you like, use the Fabric Yardage Chart on page 72 to help figure yardage.

Don't be limited by what you see here: Be your own designer. Each time you look at the designs, they will spark new thoughts. Let creativity be your guide—and have fun!

The Arrow Crown Blocks

The Arrow Crown Block

The traditional Arrow Crown block is designed around eight rows of eight squares each, commonly referred to as an 8 × 8 grid. By coloring in these 64 squares in different ways, I have designed more than 20 different blocks in this format. While I was working on these designs, especially the "bordered" D through G blocks, I noticed another design possibility: the 6 × 6 grid, or 36-square design (see page 16). These smaller blocks are still based on the Arrow Crown block, but they cannot be used with the original 8 × 8 grid block because of the size difference. There are, however, 12″ 8 × 8 grid and 9″ 6 × 6 grid blocks that I call "crossover" blocks because their size is easily adapted to use in either grid size (see page 70).

Block A*

8 × 8 grid blocks

1 square = 1½″ ▪ Finished size: 12″

These 8 × 8 grid blocks can be combined in unlimited ways to design original quilts. The designs will always look coordinated because design lines are carried from block to block. Make a very traditional quilt by combining just two blocks, or go for the unique with three to six different blocks. The L and X series of blocks are great for adding a lattice-like openness to your quilts.

The 17 Arrow Crown 8 × 8 grid blocks

Block B

Block B1*

Block C

Block C1*

Block C2

Block D

Block E

Block E1*

Block F*

Block G*

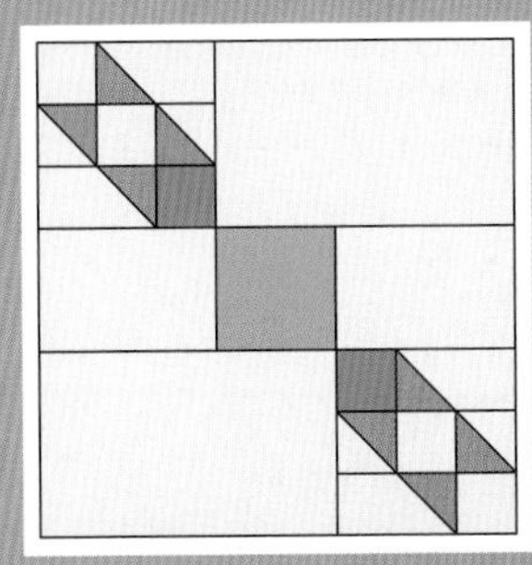

Block L*

Block L1

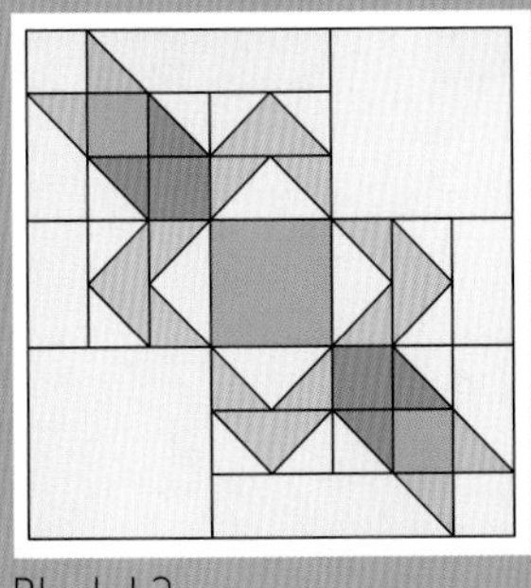

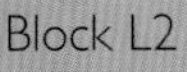

Block L2

Block X*

Block X1

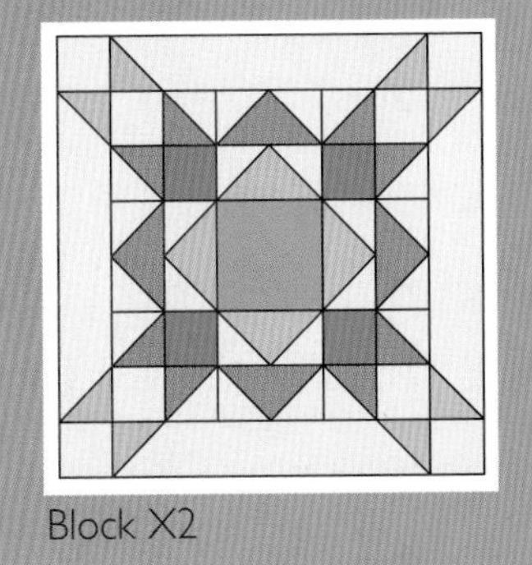

Block X2

A Block

Cutting Instructions

PIECE	COLOR	# PIECES	CUT SIZE
A		1	3½″ × 3½″
B		12	2″ × 2″
C		8	2″ × 2″
D		4	2″ × 3½″
E		4	2″ × 2″
F		4	2⅜″ × 2⅜″
G		16	2″ × 2″
H		4	2⅜″ × 2⅜″
I		4	2⅜″ × 2⅜″
J		8	2″ × 3½″
K		4	2⅜″ × 2⅜″
L		4	2″ × 2″

Piecing Instructions

Refer to page 74 for instructions for piecing the blocks using the techniques listed with the piecing diagrams below.

Step 1

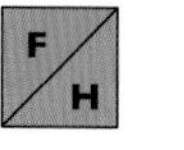

Make 8 of each half-square triangle unit.

Step 2

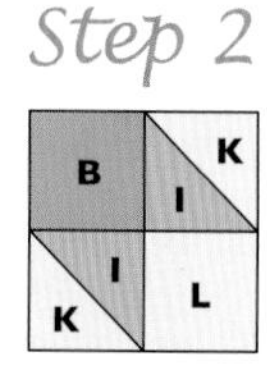

Make 4 units.

Step 3

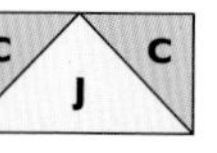

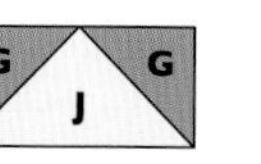

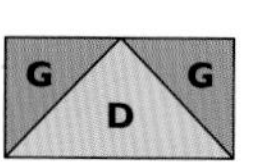

Sew and flip to make 4 of each unit.

Step 4

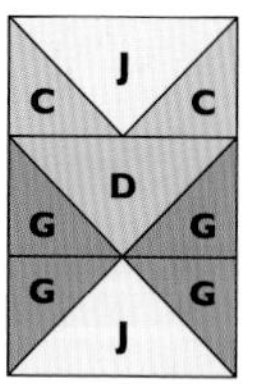

Make 4 units.

Step 5

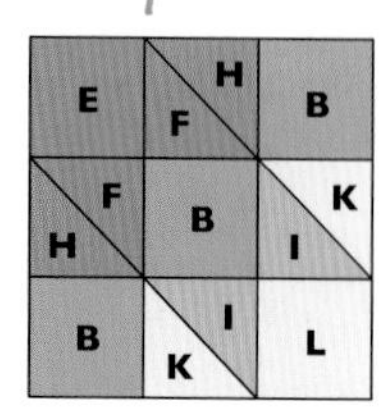

Make 4 units.

Step 6

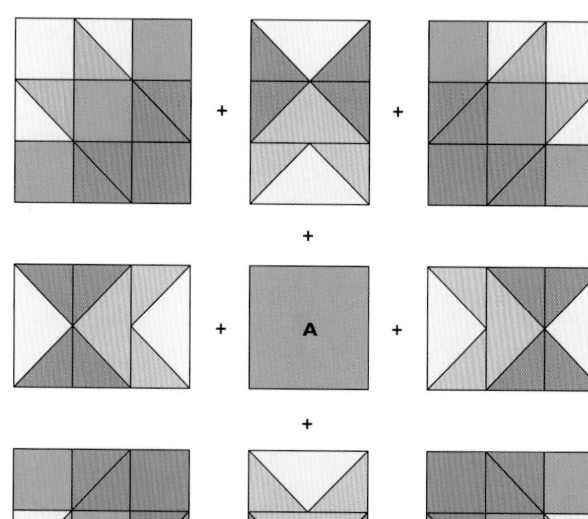

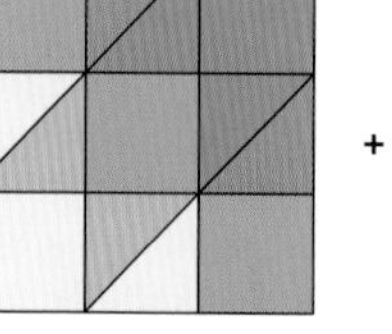

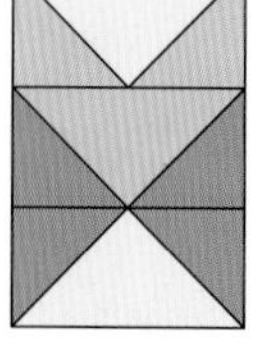

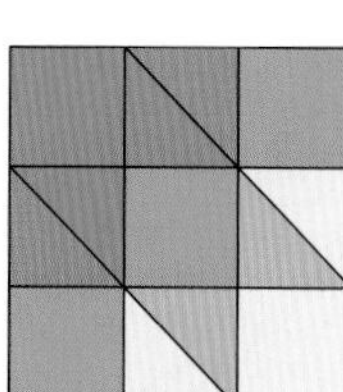

B1 Block

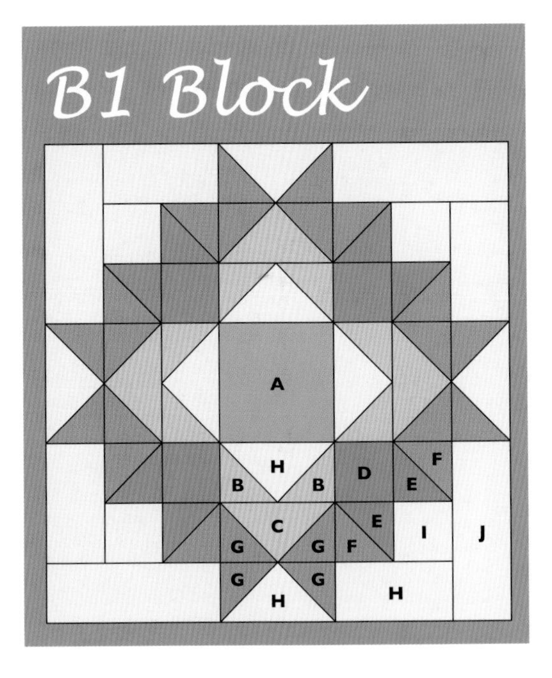

Cutting Instructions

PIECE	COLOR	# PIECES	CUT SIZE
A		1	3½″ × 3½″
B		8	2″ × 2″
C		4	2″ × 3½″
D		4	2″ × 2″
E		4	2⅜″ × 2⅜″
F		4	2⅜″ × 2⅜″
G		16	2″ × 2″
H		12	2″ × 3½″
I		4	2″ × 2″
J		4	2″ × 5″

Piecing Instructions

Refer to page 74 for instructions for piecing the blocks using the techniques listed with the piecing diagrams below.

Step 1

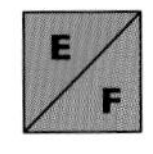

Make 8 half-square triangle units.

Step 2

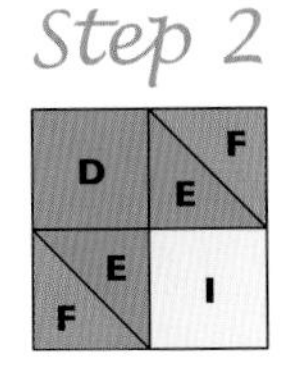

Make 4 units.

Step 3

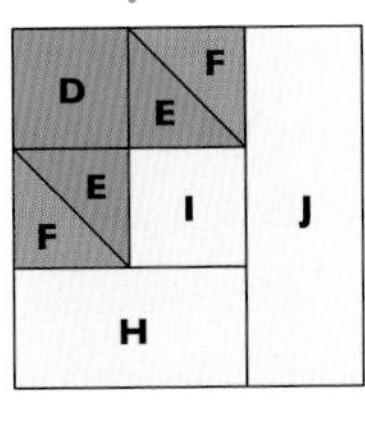

Make 4 units.

Step 4

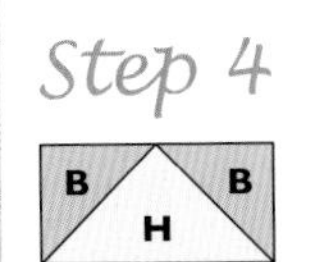

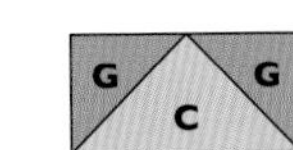

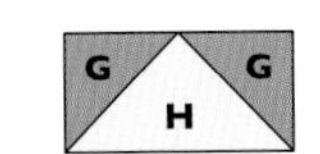

Sew and flip to make 4 of each unit.

Step 5

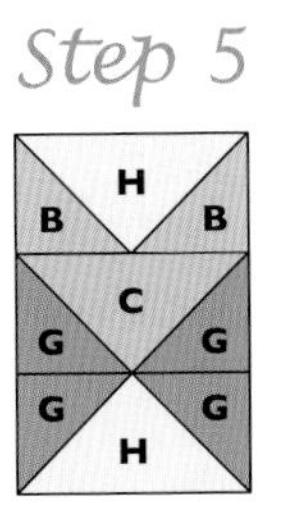

Make 4 units.

Step 6

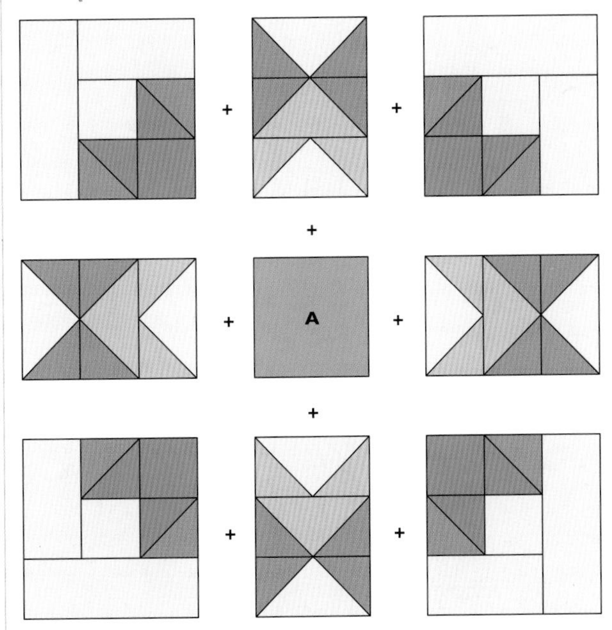

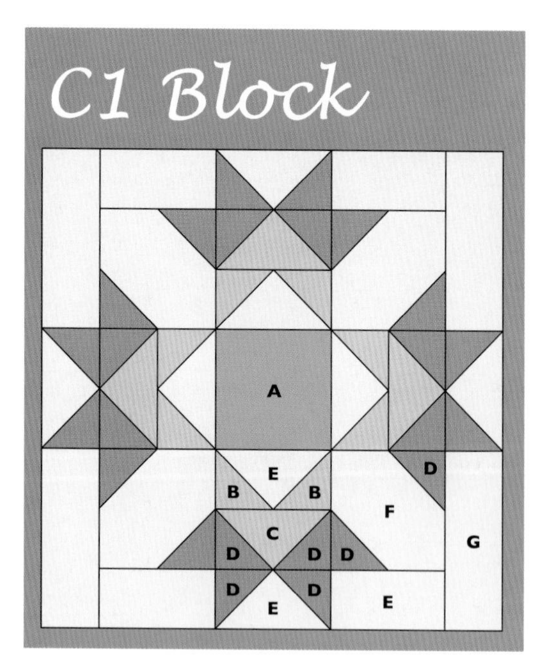

Cutting Instructions

PIECE	COLOR	# PIECES	CUT SIZE
A		1	3½″ × 3½″
B		8	2″ × 2″
C		4	2″ × 3½″
D		24	2″ × 2″
E		12	2″ × 3½″
F		4	3½″ × 3½″
G		4	2″ × 5″

Piecing Instructions

Refer to page 74 for instructions for piecing the blocks using the techniques listed with the piecing diagrams below.

Step 1

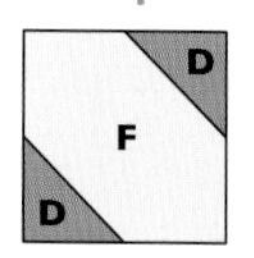

Sew and flip to make 4 units.

Step 2

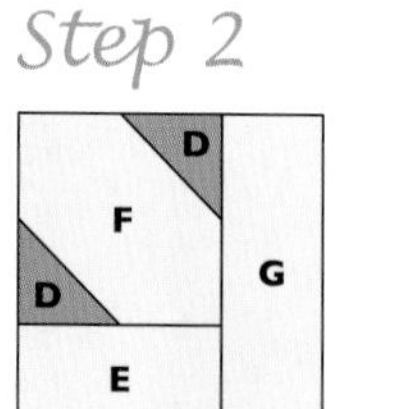

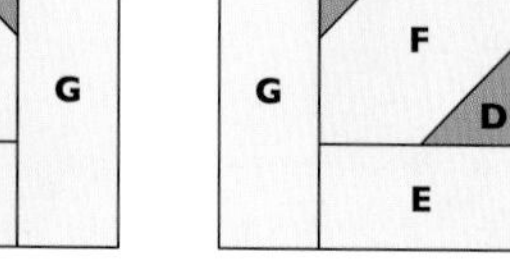

Make 2 of each unit.

Step 3

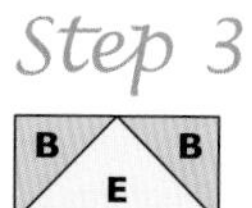

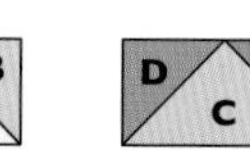

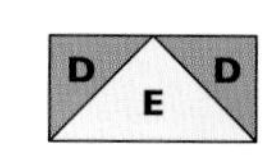

Sew and flip to make 4 of each unit.

Step 4

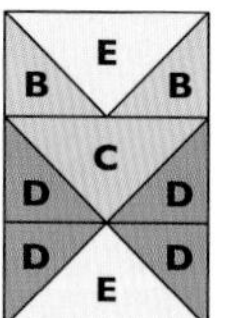

Make 4 units.

Step 5

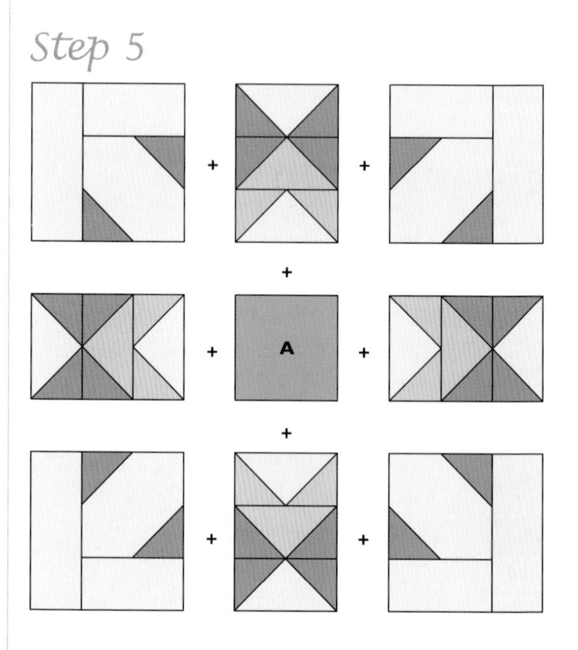

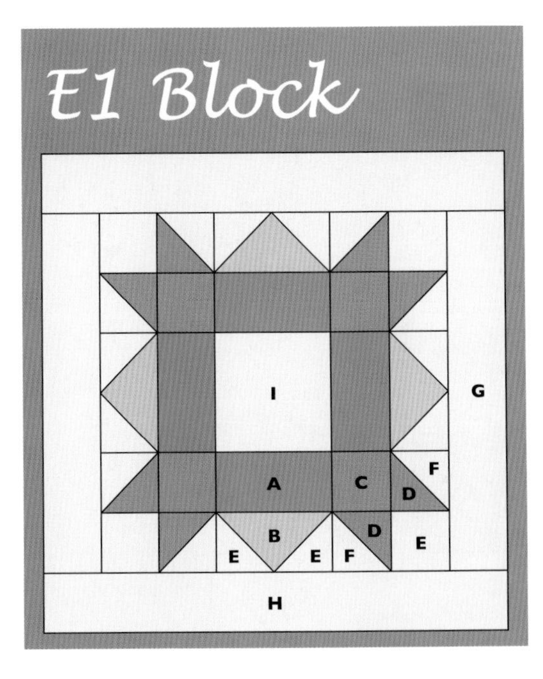

Cutting Instructions

PIECE	COLOR	# PIECES	CUT SIZE
A		4	2″ × 3½″
B		4	2″ × 3½″
C		4	2″ × 2″
D		4	2⅜″ × 2⅜″
E		12	2″ × 2″
F		4	2⅜″ × 2⅜″
G		2	2″ × 9½″
H		2	2″ × 12½″
I		1	3½″ × 3½″

Piecing Instructions

Refer to page 74 for instructions for piecing the blocks using the techniques listed with the piecing diagrams below.

Step 1

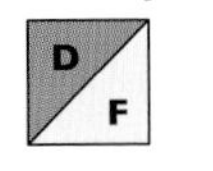

Make 8 half-square triangle units.

Step 2

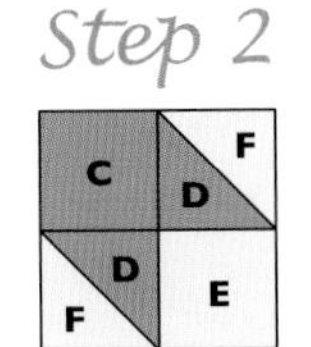

Make 4 units.

Step 3

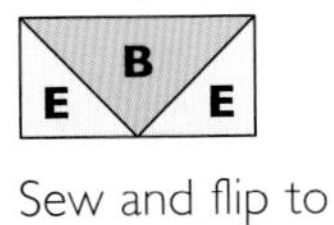

Sew and flip to make 4 units.

Step 4

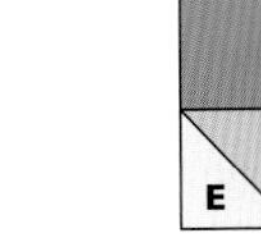

Make 4 units.

Step 5

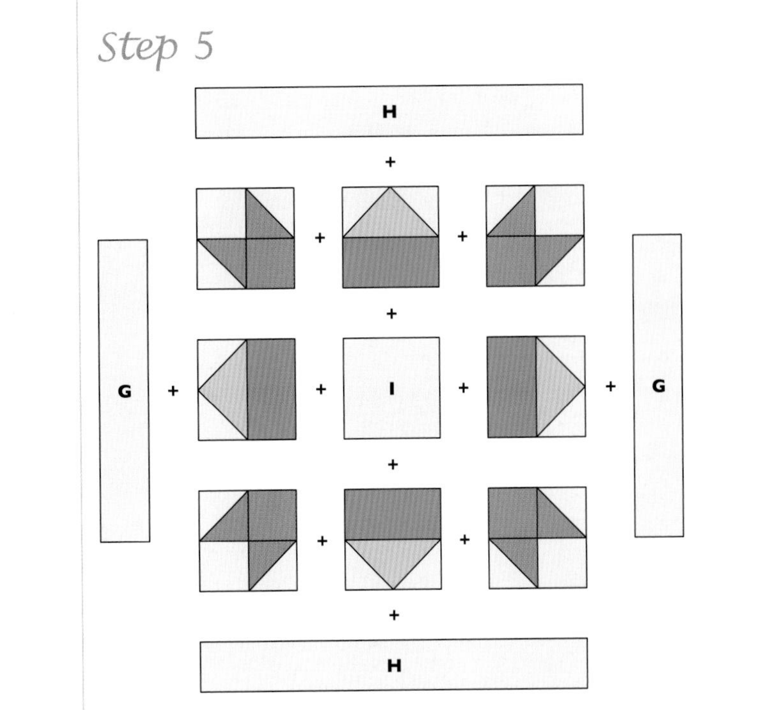

Cutting Instructions

PIECE	COLOR	# PIECES	CUT SIZE
A		1	3½″ × 3½″
B		4	2″ × 3½″
C		12	2″ × 2″
D		4	3½″ × 6½″
E		8	2″ × 2″
F		4	3½″ × 3½″

Piecing Instructions

Refer to page 74 for instructions for piecing the blocks using the techniques listed with the piecing diagrams below.

Step 1

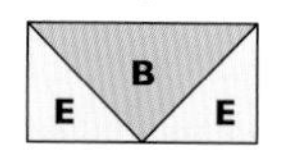

Sew and flip to make 4 units.

Step 2

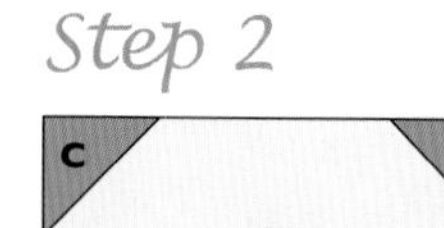

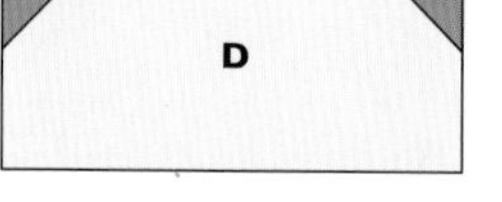

Sew and flip to make 4 units.

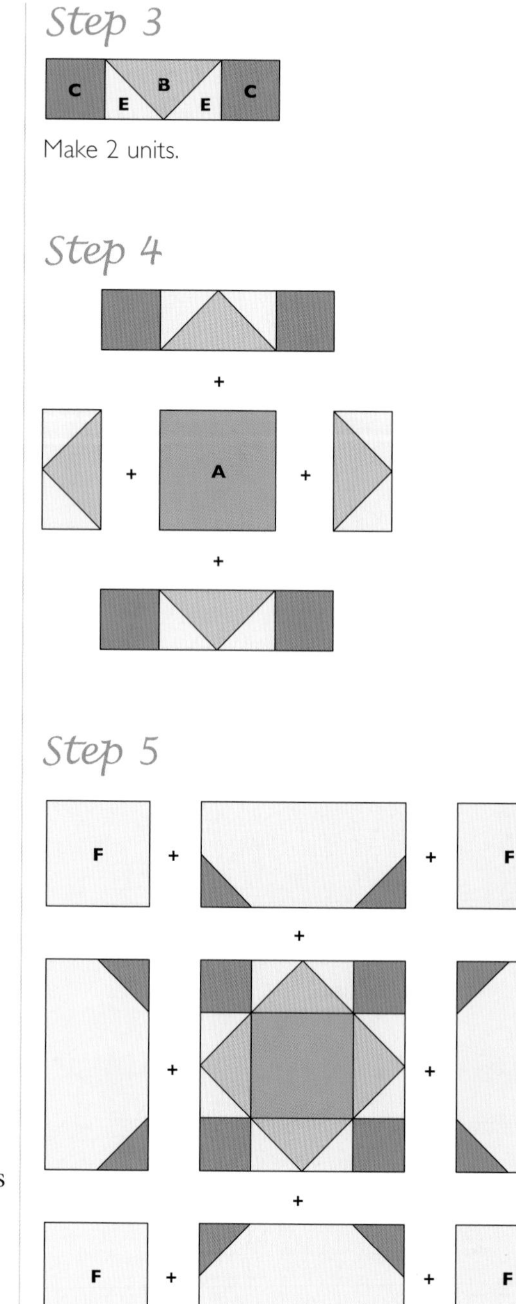

Cutting Instructions

PIECE	COLOR	# PIECES	CUT SIZE
A		1	3½″ x 3½″
B		4	2″ x 3½″
C		8	2″ x 2″
D		4	2⅜″ x 2⅜″
E		8	2″ x 3½″
F		4	2⅜″ x 2⅜″
G		8	2″ x 2″
H		2	2″ x 9½″
I		2	2″ x 12½″

Piecing Instructions

Refer to page 74 for instructions for piecing the blocks using the techniques listed with the piecing diagrams below.

Step 1

Make 8 half-square triangle units.

Step 2

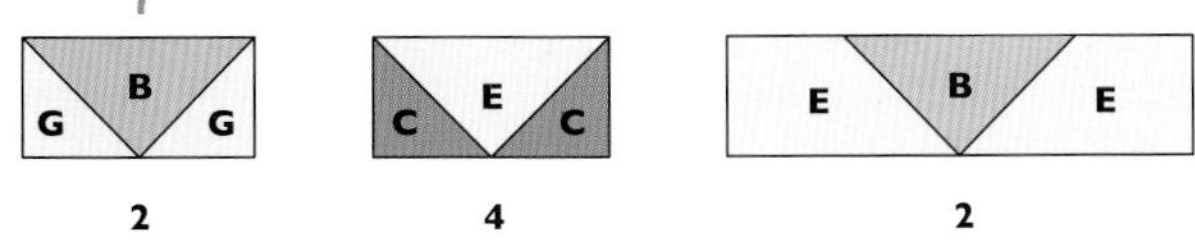

Sew and flip to make 2 GBG units, 4 CEC units, and 2 EBE units.

Step 3

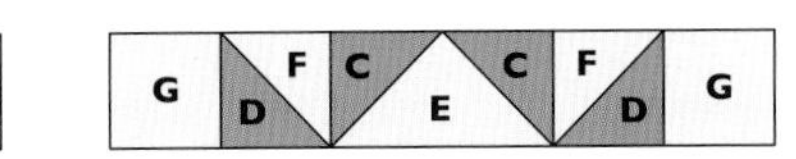

Make 2 of each unit.

Step 4

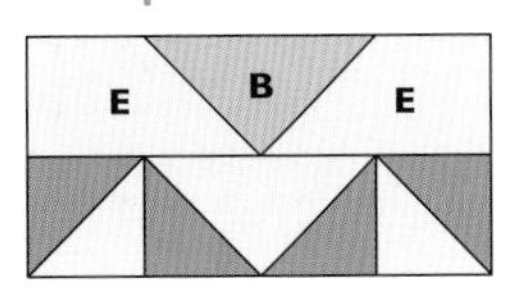

Make 2 units.

Step 5

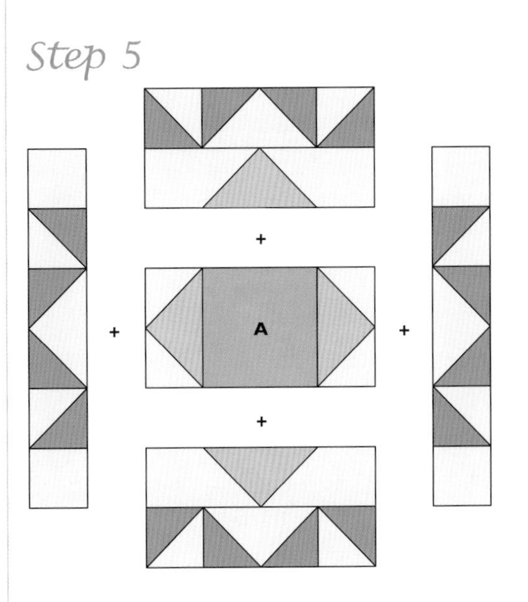

Step 6

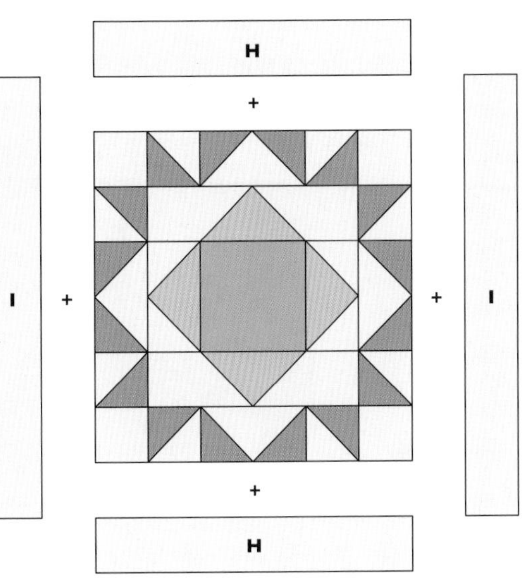

L Block

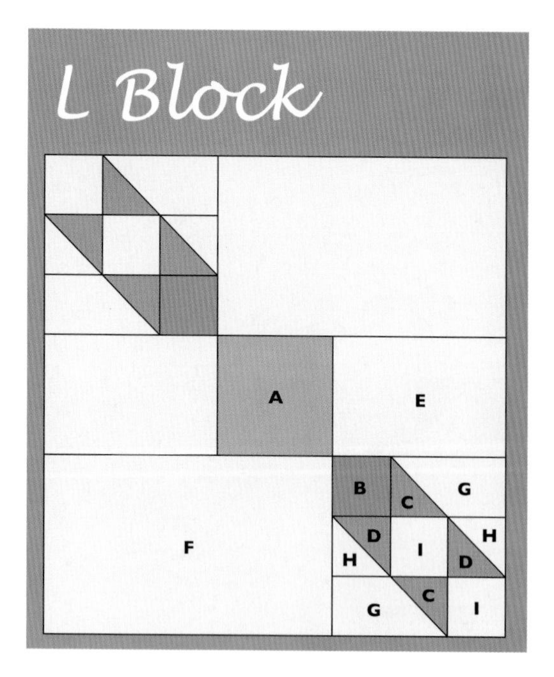

Cutting Instructions

PIECE	COLOR	# PIECES	CUT SIZE
A		1	3½″ × 3½″
B		2	2″ × 2″
C		4	2″ × 2″
D		2	2⅜″ × 2⅜″
E		2	3½″ × 5″
F		2	5″ × 8″
G		4	2″ × 3½″
H		2	2⅜″ × 2⅜″
I		4	2″ × 2″

Piecing Instructions

Refer to page 74 for instructions for piecing the blocks using the techniques listed with the piecing diagrams below.

Make 4 HD half-square triangle units; sew and flip to make 4 GC units.

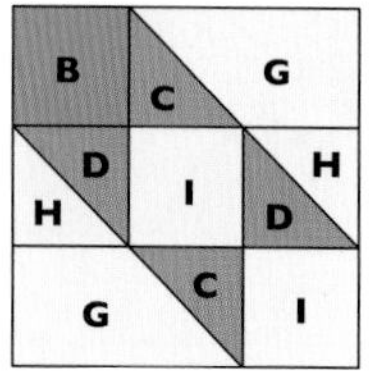

Make 2 units.

Step 3

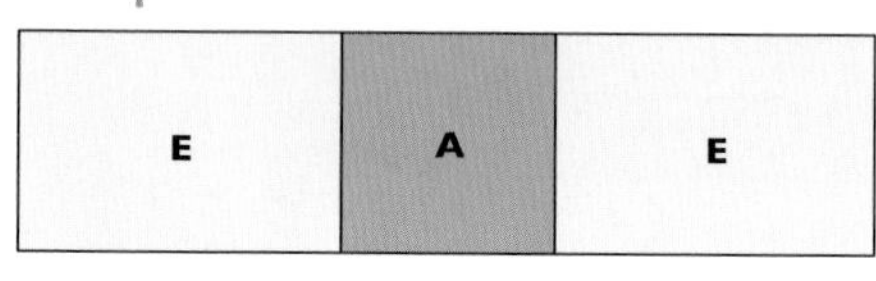

Make 1 unit.

Step 4

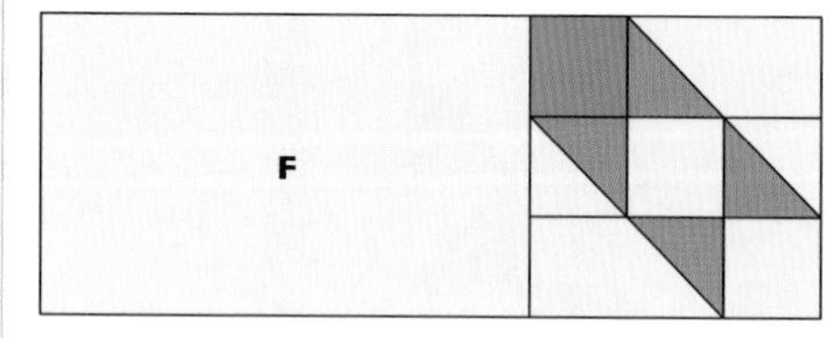

Make 2 units.

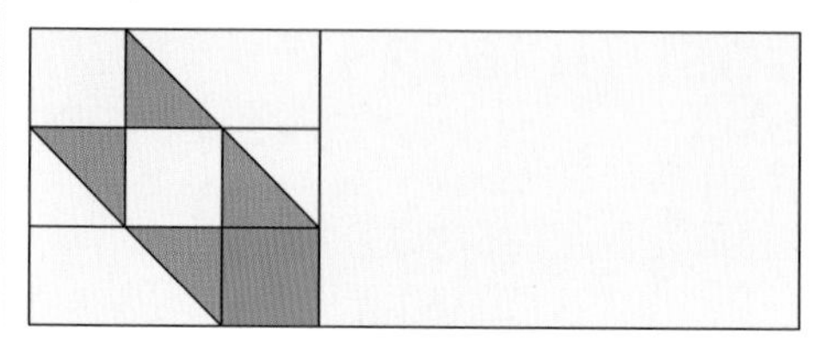

+

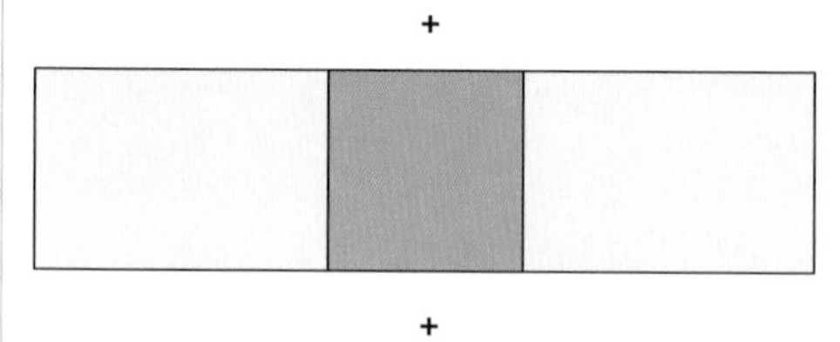

+

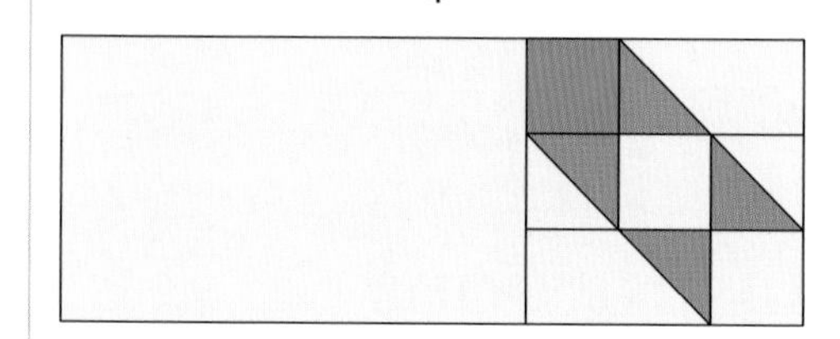

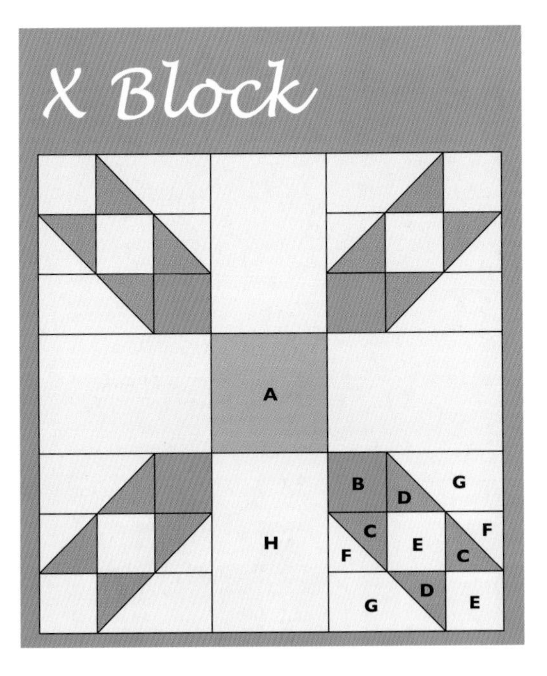

Cutting Instructions

PIECE	COLOR	# PIECES	CUT SIZE
A		1	3½″ × 3½″
B		4	2″ × 2″
C		4	2⅜″ × 2⅜″
D		8	2″ × 2″
E		8	2″ × 2″
F		4	2⅜″ × 2⅜″
G		8	2″ × 3½″
H		4	3½″ × 5″

Piecing Instructions

Refer to page 74 for instructions for piecing the blocks using the techniques listed with the piecing diagrams below.

Step 1

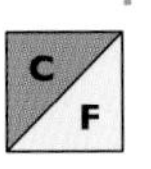

Make 8 half-square triangle units.

Step 2

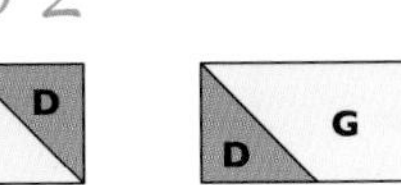

Sew and flip to make 4 of each unit.

Step 3

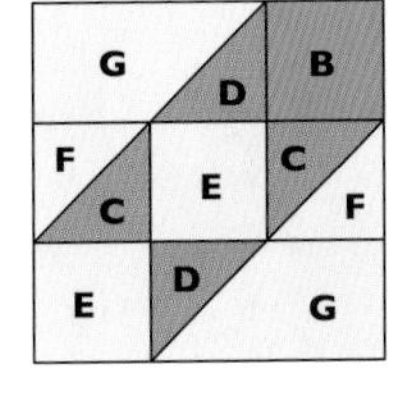

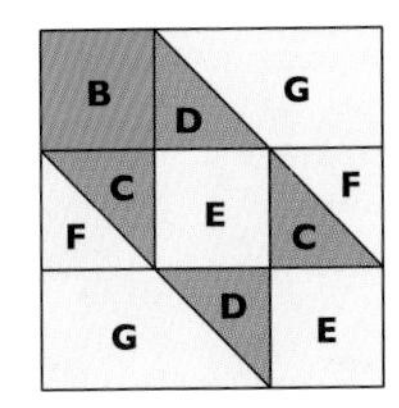

Make 2 of each unit.

Step 4

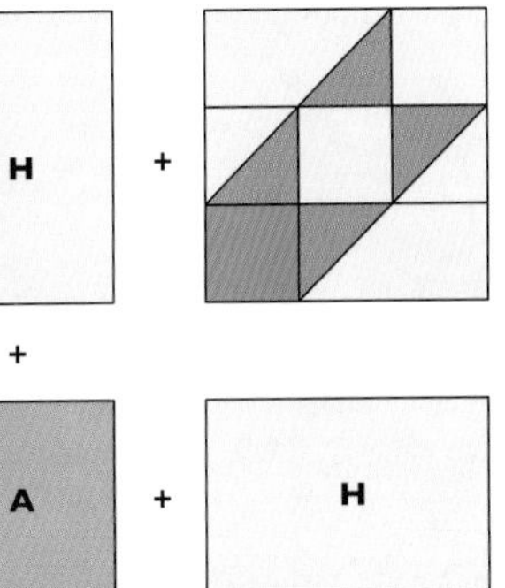

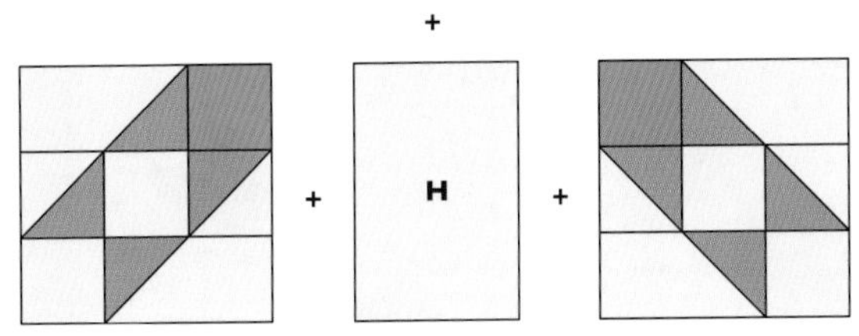

6 x 6 Grid Blocks

1 square = 1½″ ▪ Finished size: 9″

These 18 blocks are just some of the variations that can be found in the Arrow Crown block. The design possibilities are endless. See *Lavender Sachet* on page 60 to see 4 A1 blocks placed together.

The 18 Arrow Crown 6x6 grid blocks

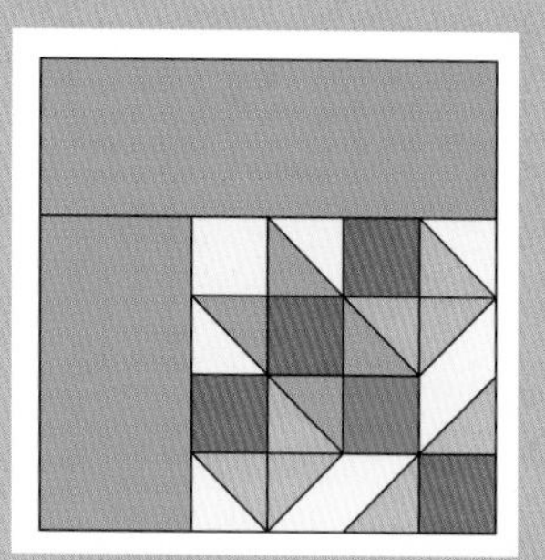
Block A1*

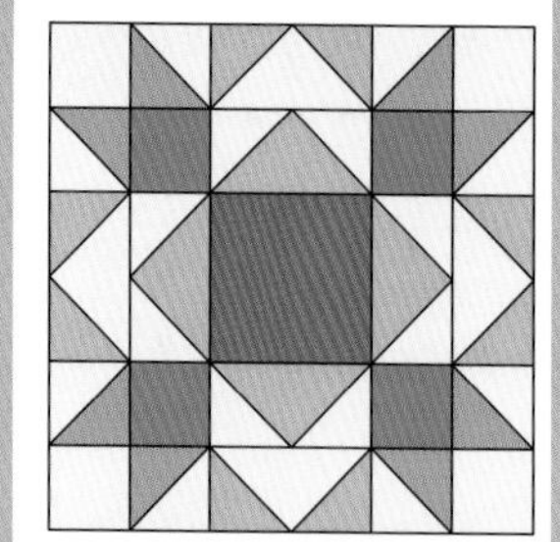
Block H

Block H1*

Block I*

Block J*

Block K*

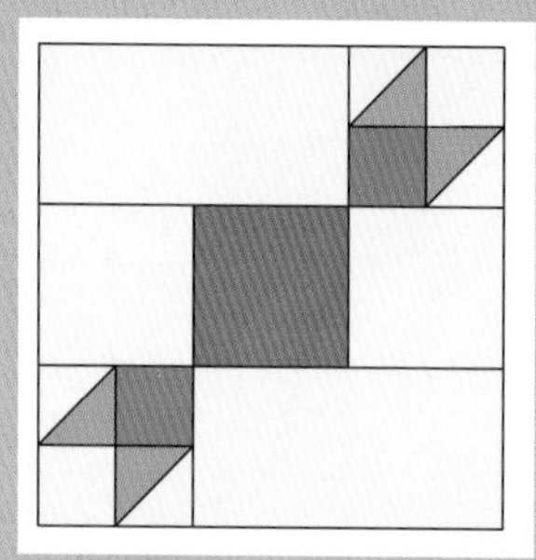
Block L3*

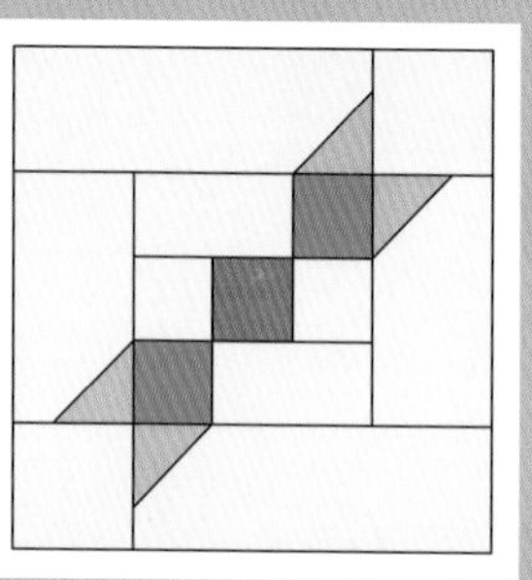
Block L4*

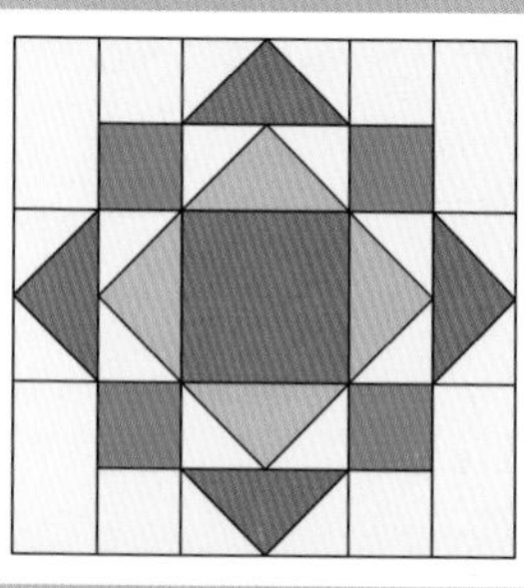
Block M

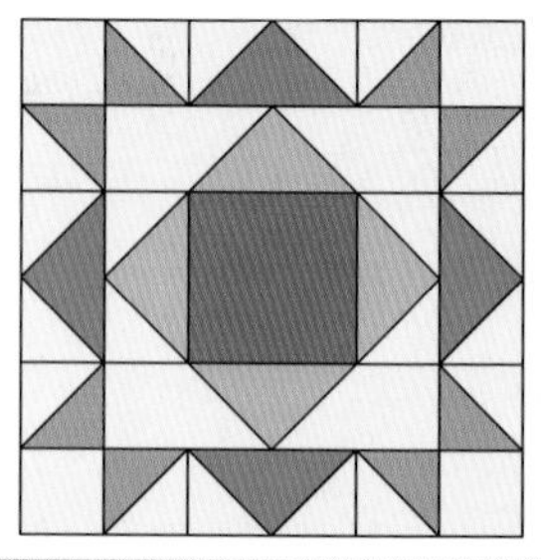
Block N*

Block N1

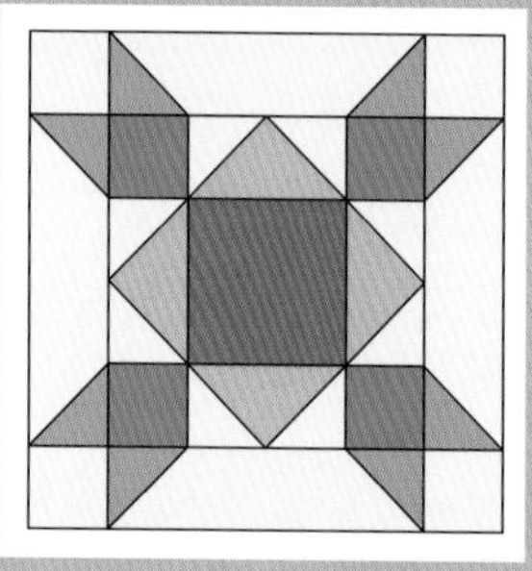
Block O*

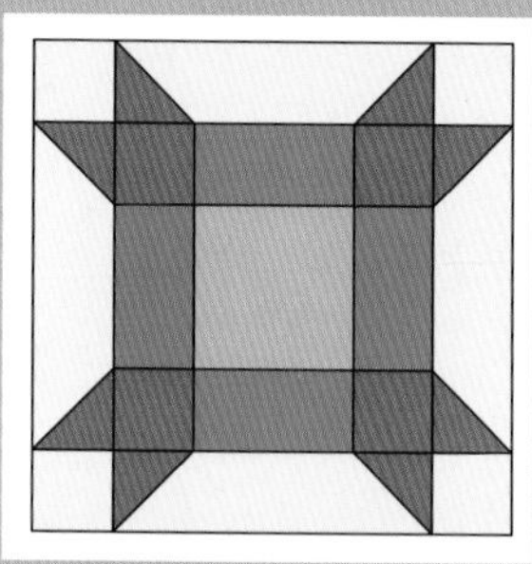
Block P

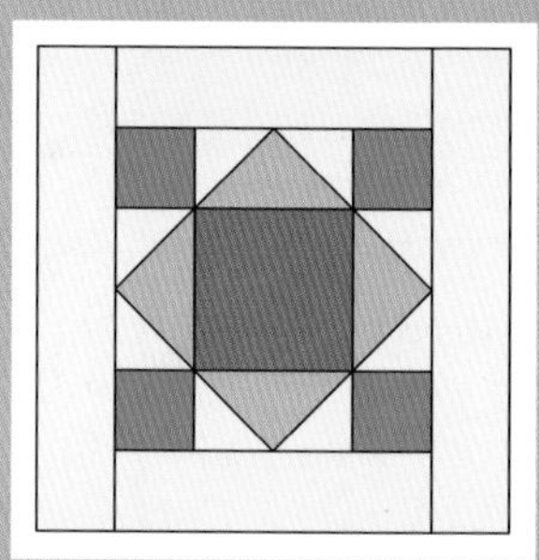
Block Q

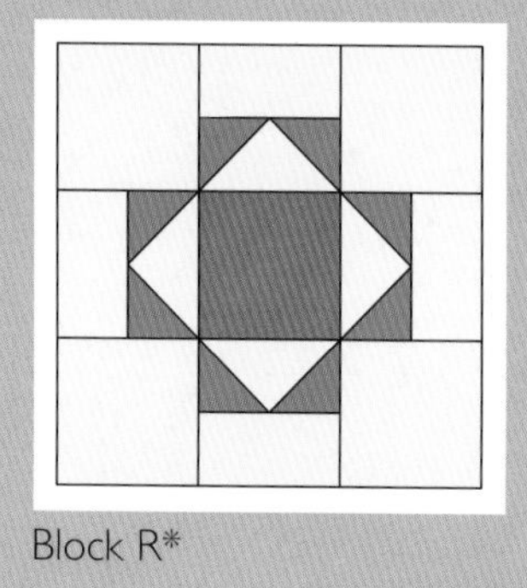
Block R*

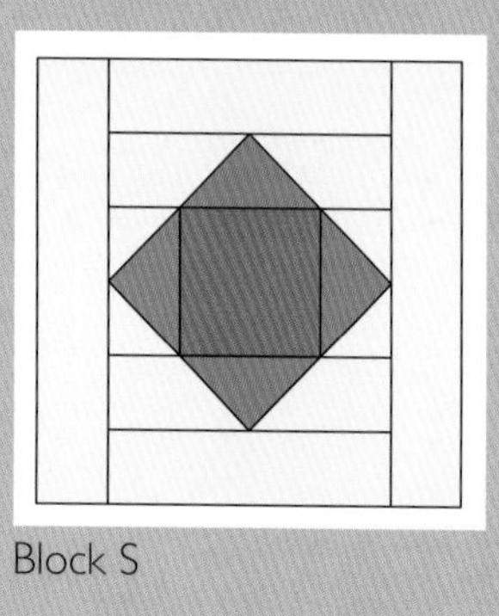
Block S

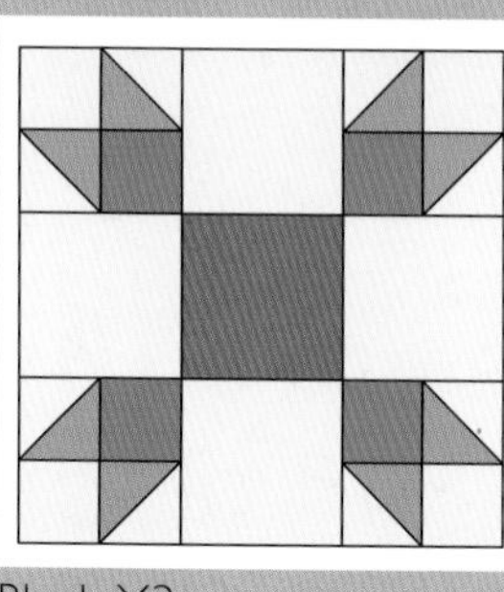
Block X3

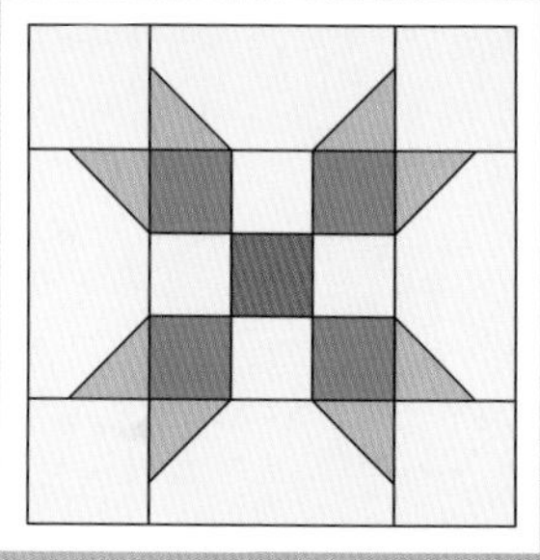
Block X4*

* An asterisk denotes the block is used in a project quilt

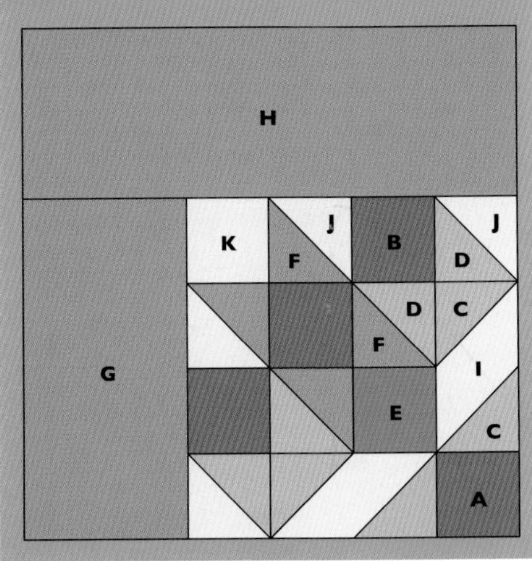

Cutting Instructions

PIECE	COLOR	# PIECES	CUT SIZE
A		1	2″ × 2″
B		3	2″ × 2″
C		4	2″ × 2″
D		2	2⅜″ × 2⅜″
E		1	2″ × 2″
F		2	2⅜″ × 2⅜″
G		1	3½″ × 6½″
H		1	3½″ × 9½″
I		2	2″ × 3½″
J		2	2⅜″ × 2⅜″
K		1	2″ × 2″

Piecing Instructions

Refer to page 74 for instructions for piecing the blocks using the techniques listed with the piecing diagrams below.

Step 1

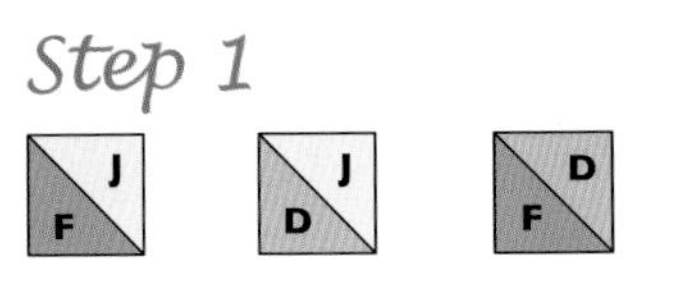

Make 2 half-square triangle units of each.

Step 2

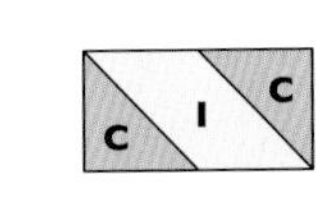

Sew and flip to make 1 of each unit.

Step 3

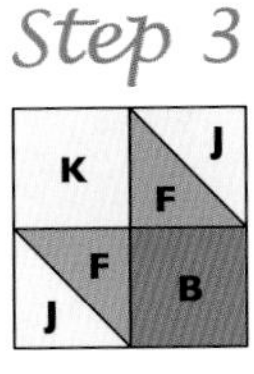

Make 1 unit.

Step 4

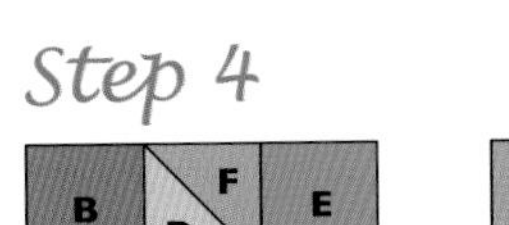

Make 1 unit of each color set.

Step 5

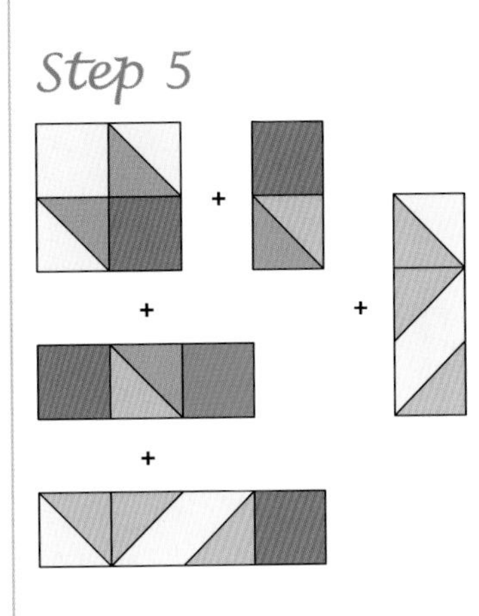

Step 6

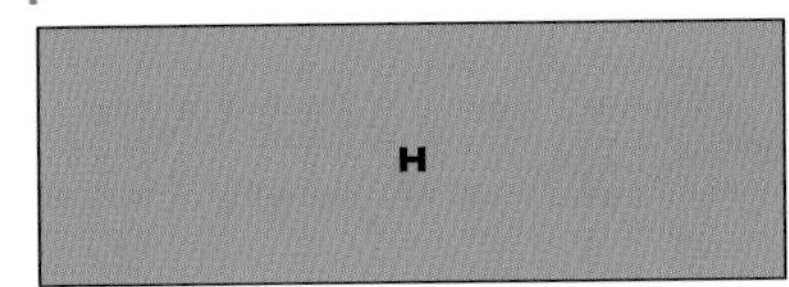

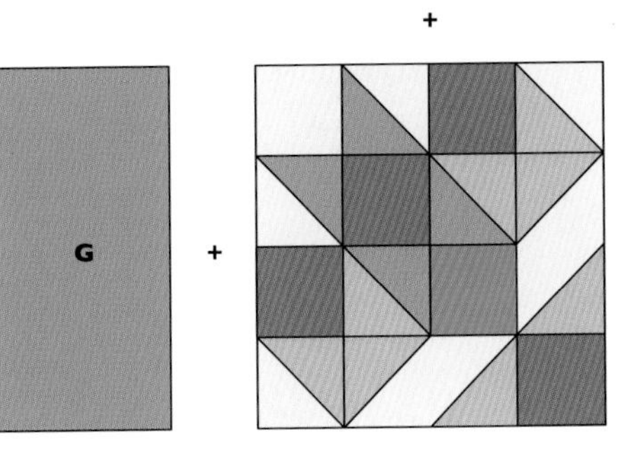

Cutting Instructions

PIECE	COLOR	# PIECES	CUT SIZE
A		1	3½″ × 3½″
B		8	2″ × 2″
C		4	2″ × 3½″
D		4	2″ × 2″
E		4	2⅜″ × 2⅜″
F		4	2″ × 3½″
G		12	2″ × 2″
H		4	2⅜″ × 2⅜″

Piecing Instructions

Refer to page 74 for instructions for piecing the blocks using the techniques listed with the piecing diagrams below.

Step 1

E
H

Make 8 half-square triangle units.

Step 2

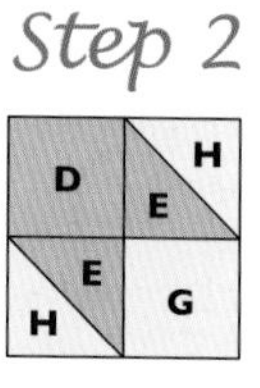

Make 4 units.

Step 3

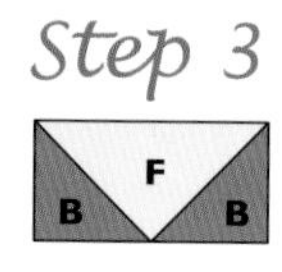

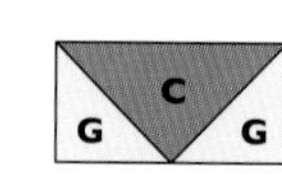

Sew and flip to make 4 of each unit.

Step 4

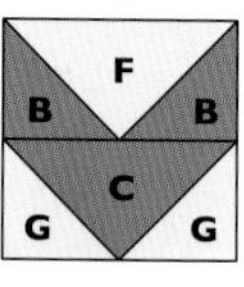

Make 4 units.

Step 5

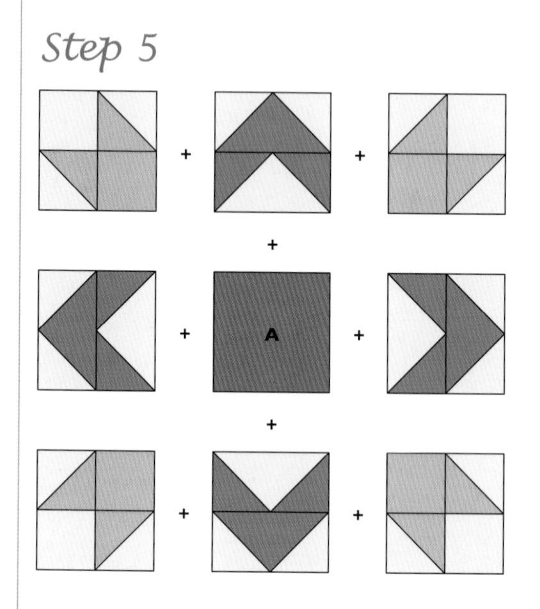

Cutting Instructions

PIECE	COLOR	# PIECES	CUT SIZE
A		1	3½″ × 3½″
B		4	2″ × 3½″
C		4	2″ × 3½″
D		4	2⅜″ × 2⅜″
E		4	2″ × 2″
F		20	2″ × 2″
G		4	2⅜″ × 2⅜″

Piecing Instructions

Refer to page 74 for instructions for piecing the blocks using the techniques listed with the piecing diagrams below.

Step 1

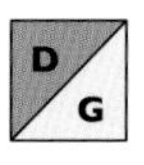

Make 8 half-square triangle units.

Step 2

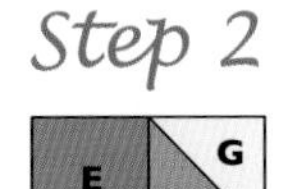

Make 4 units.

Step 3

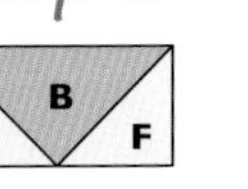

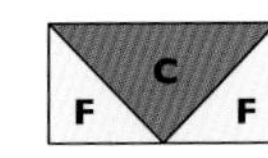

Sew and flip to make 4 of each unit.

Step 4

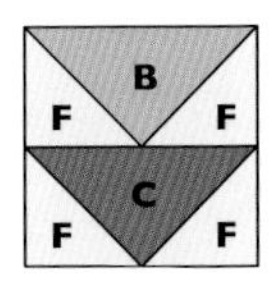

Make 4 units.

Step 5

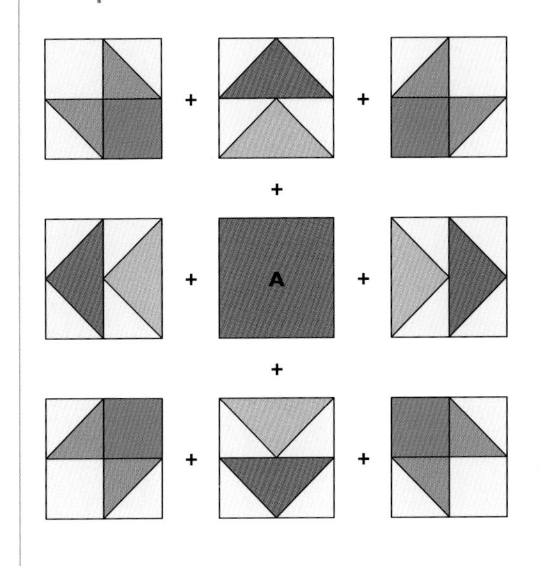

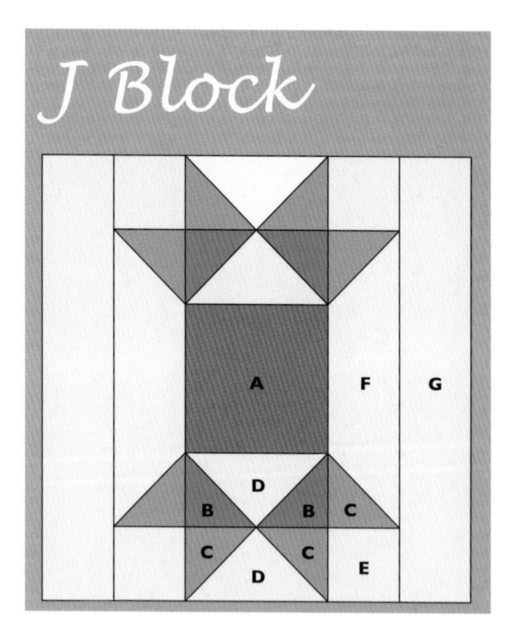

Cutting Instructions

PIECE	COLOR	# PIECES	CUT SIZE
A		1	3½″ × 3½″
B		4	2″ × 2″
C		8	2″ × 2″
D		4	2″ × 3½″
E		4	2″ × 2″
F		2	2″ × 6½″
G		2	2″ × 9½″

Piecing Instructions

Refer to page 74 for instructions for piecing the blocks using the techniques listed with the piecing diagrams below.

Step 1

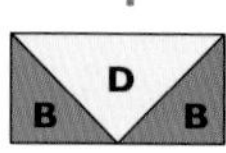

C D C

Sew and flip to make 2 of each unit.

Step 2

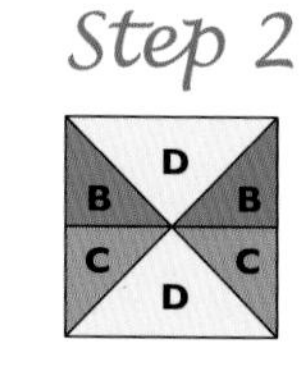

Make 2 units.

Step 3

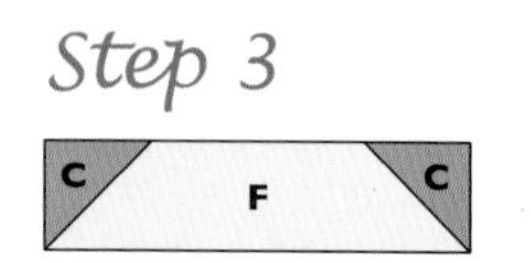

Sew and flip to make 2 units.

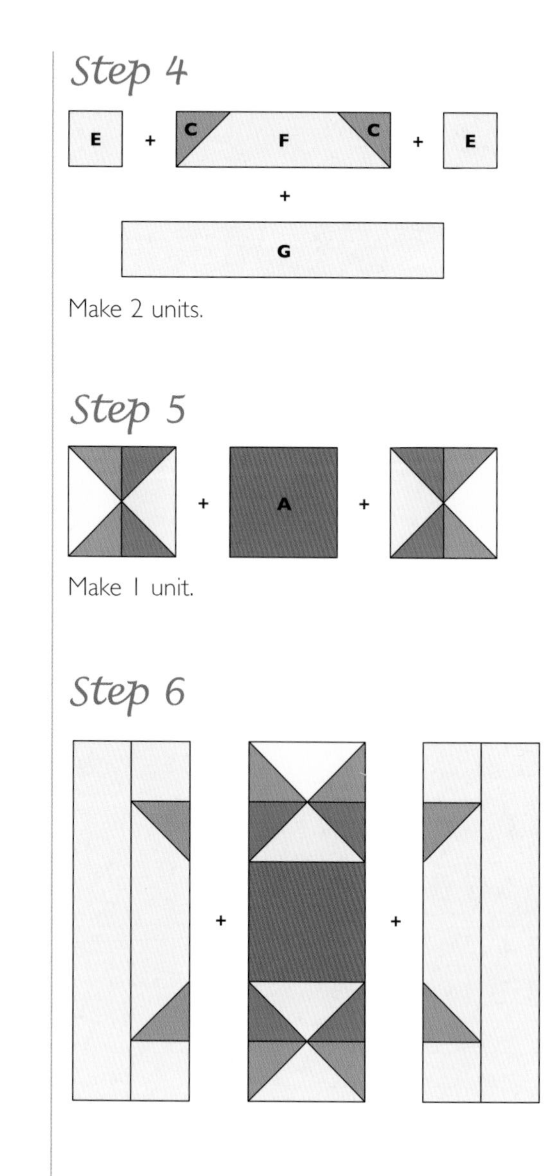

Cutting Instructions

PIECE	COLOR	# PIECES	CUT SIZE
A		1	3½″ × 3½″
B		8	2″ × 2″
C		8	2″ × 2″
D		4	2″ × 2″
E		12	2″ × 3½″
F		4	2″ × 2″

Piecing Instructions

Refer to page 74 for instructions for piecing the blocks using the techniques listed with the piecing diagrams below.

Step 1

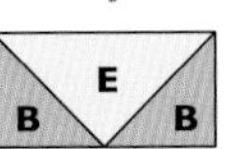

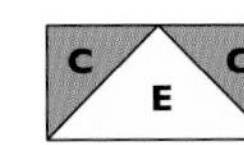

Sew and flip to make 4 of each unit.

Step 2

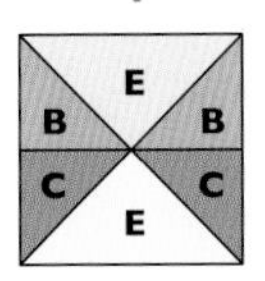

Make 4 units.

Step 3

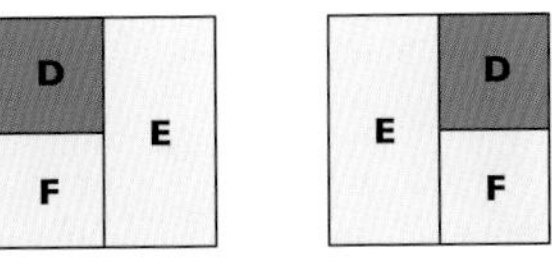

Make 2 of each unit.

Step 4

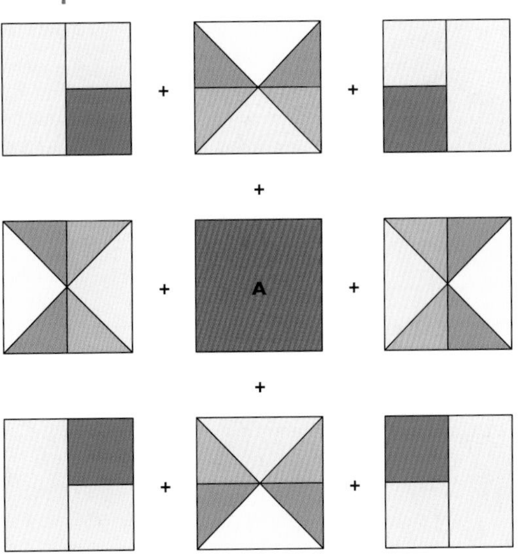

L3 Block

Cutting Instructions

PIECE	COLOR	# PIECES	CUT SIZE
A		1	3½″ × 3½″
B		2	2″ × 2″
C		2	2⅜″ × 2⅜″
D		2	2⅜″ × 2⅜″
E		2	2″ × 2″
F		2	3½″ × 3½″
G		2	3½″ × 6½″

Piecing Instructions

Refer to page 74 for instructions for piecing the blocks using the techniques listed with the piecing diagrams below.

Step 1

Make 4 half-square triangle units.

Step 2

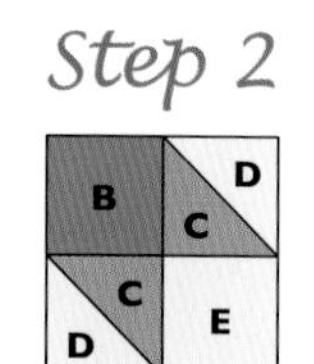

Make 2 units.

Step 3

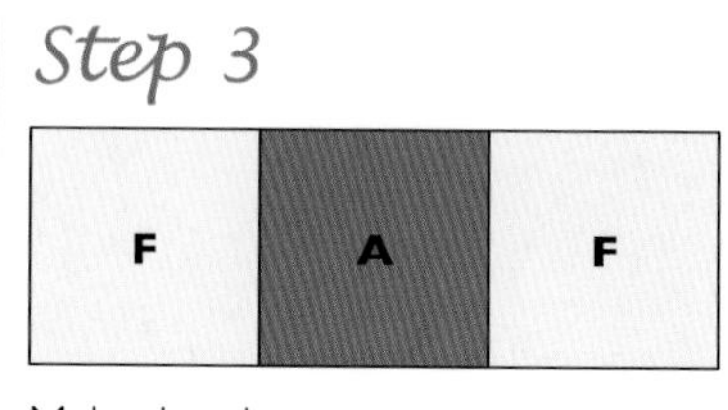

Make 1 unit.

Step 4

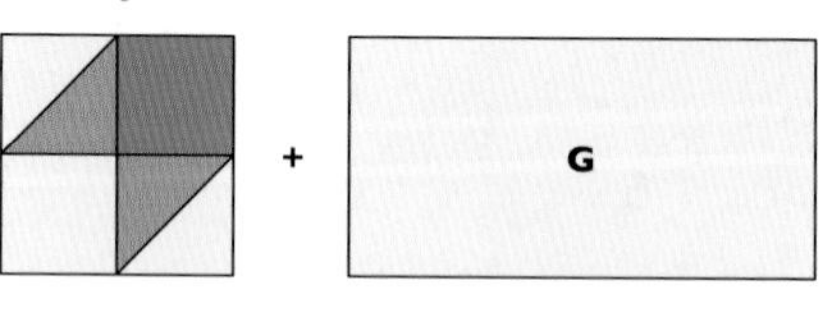

Make 2 units.

Step 5

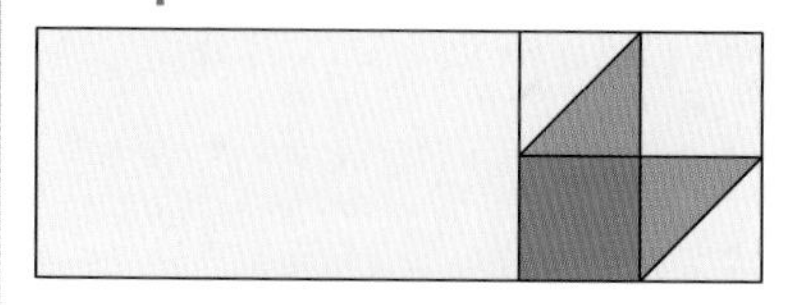

+

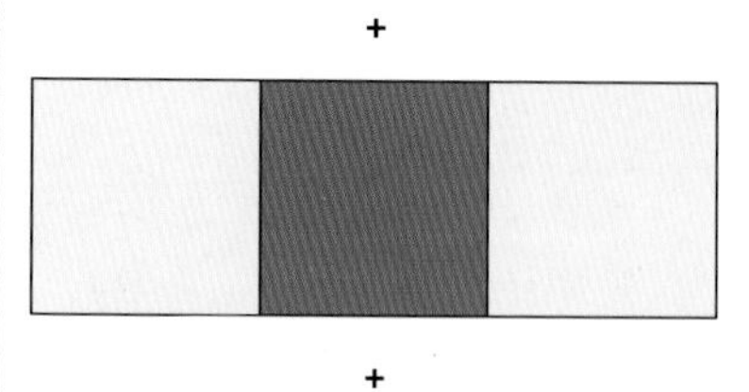

+

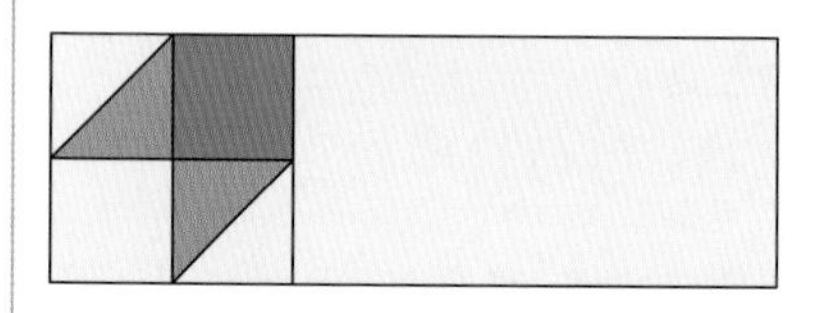

L4 Block

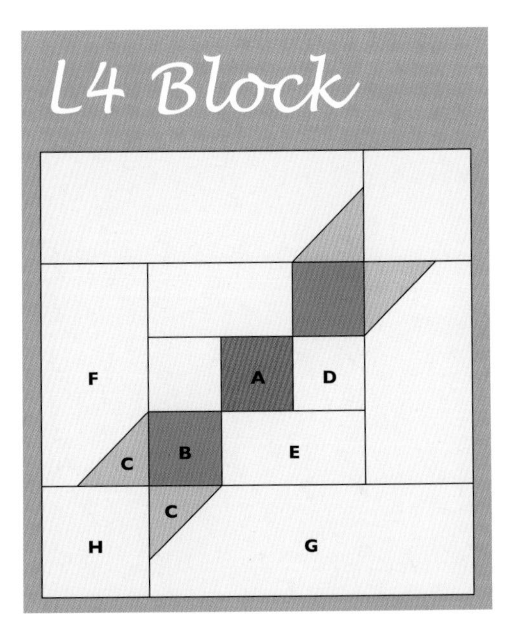

Cutting Instructions

PIECE	COLOR	# PIECES	CUT SIZE
A		1	2″ × 2″
B		2	2″ × 2″
C		4	2″ × 2″
D		2	2″ × 2″
E		2	2″ × 3½″
F		2	2¾″ × 5″
G		2	2¾″ × 7¼″
H		2	2¾″ × 2¾″

Piecing Instructions

Refer to page 74 for instructions for piecing the blocks using the techniques listed with the piecing diagrams below.

Step 1

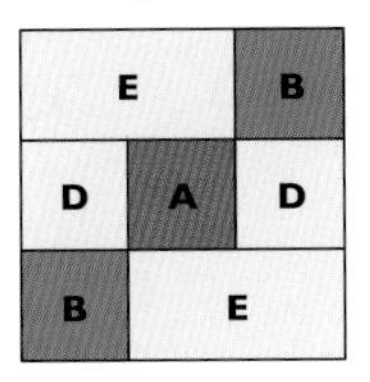

Make 1 unit.

Step 2

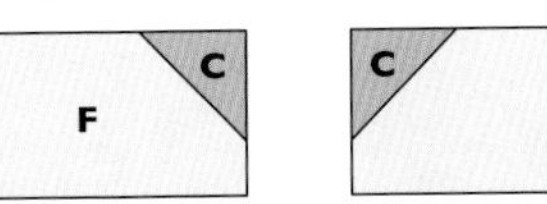

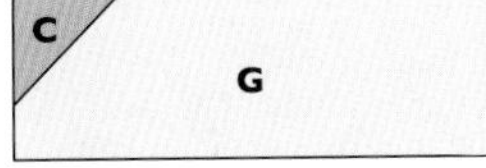

Sew and flip to make 2 of each unit.

Step 3

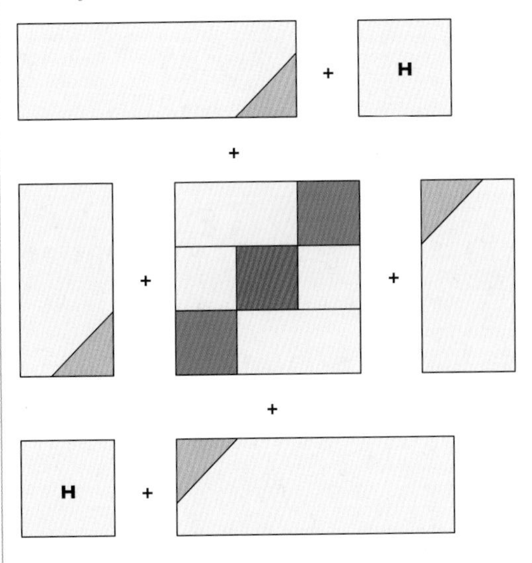

Cutting Instructions

PIECE	COLOR	# PIECES	CUT SIZE
A		1	3½″ × 3½″
B		4	2″ × 3½″
C		4	2″ × 3½″
D		4	2⅜″ × 2⅜″
E		4	2″ × 3½″
F		16	2″ × 2″
G		4	2⅜″ × 2⅜″

Piecing Instructions

Refer to page 74 for instructions for piecing the blocks using the techniques listed with the piecing diagrams below.

Step 1

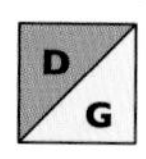

Make 8 half-square triangle units.

Step 2

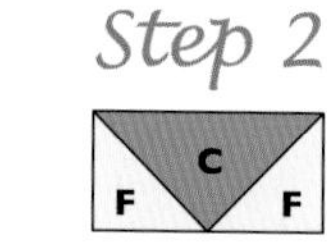

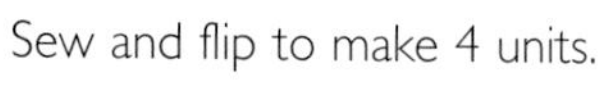
Sew and flip to make 4 units.

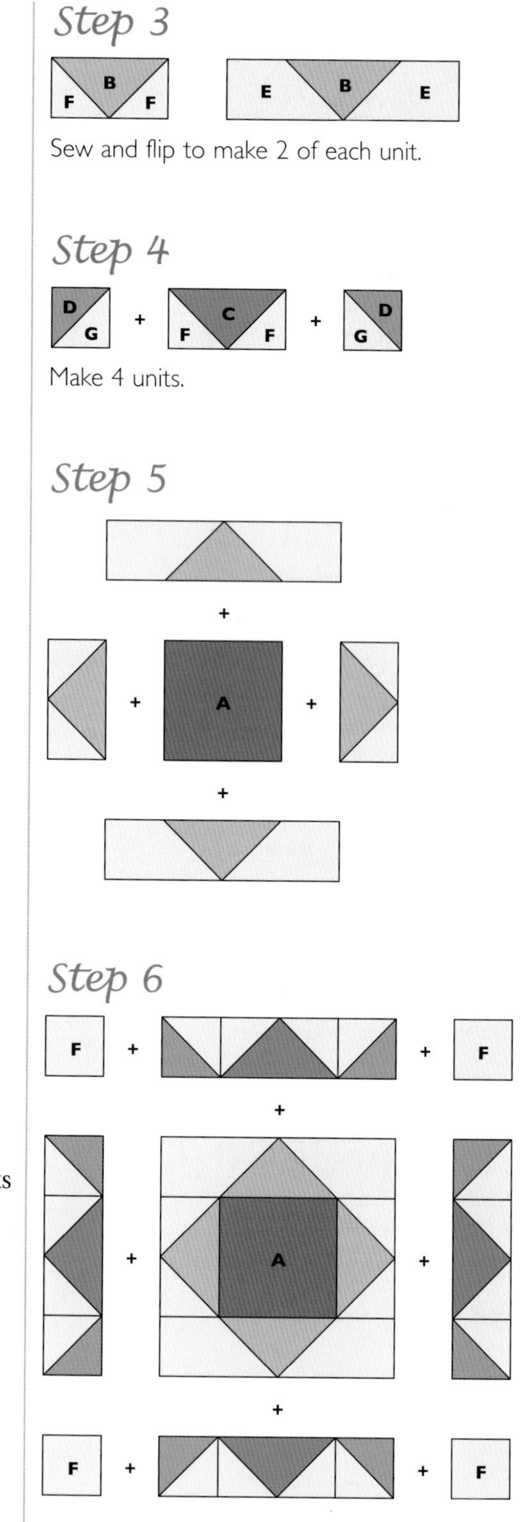

O Block

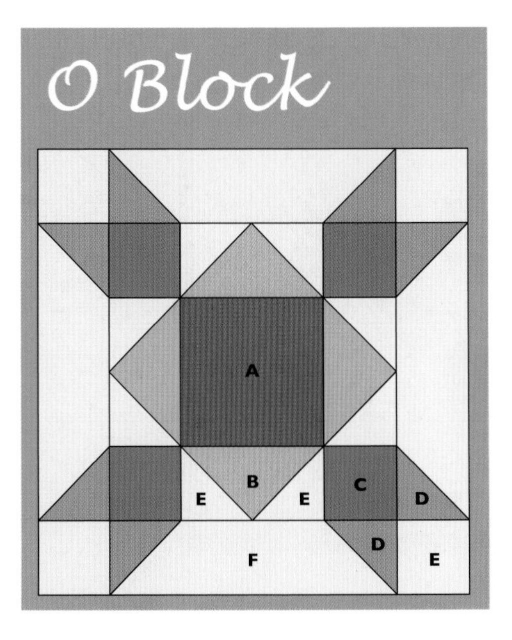

Cutting Instructions

PIECE	COLOR	# PIECES	CUT SIZE
A		1	3½″ × 3½″
B		4	2″ × 3½″
C		4	2″ × 2″
D		8	2″ × 2″
E		12	2″ × 2″
F		4	2″ × 6½″

Piecing Instructions

Refer to page 74 for instructions for piecing the blocks using the techniques listed with the piecing diagrams below.

Step 1

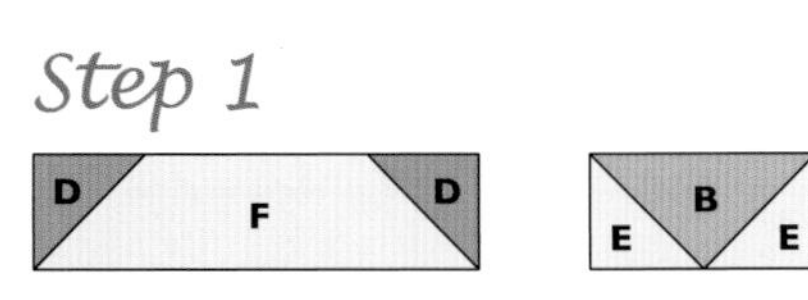

Sew and flip to make 4 of each unit.

Step 2

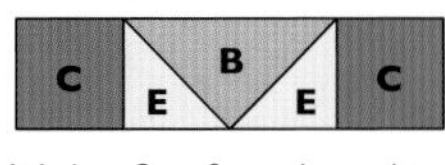

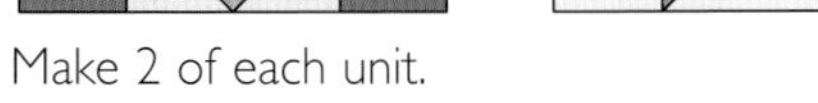

Make 2 of each unit.

Step 3

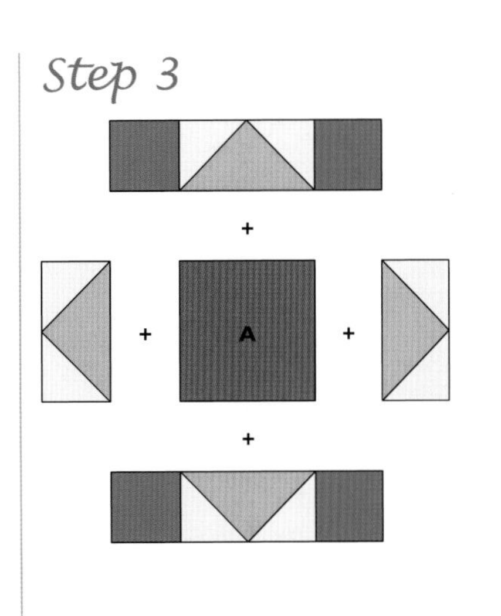

Step 4

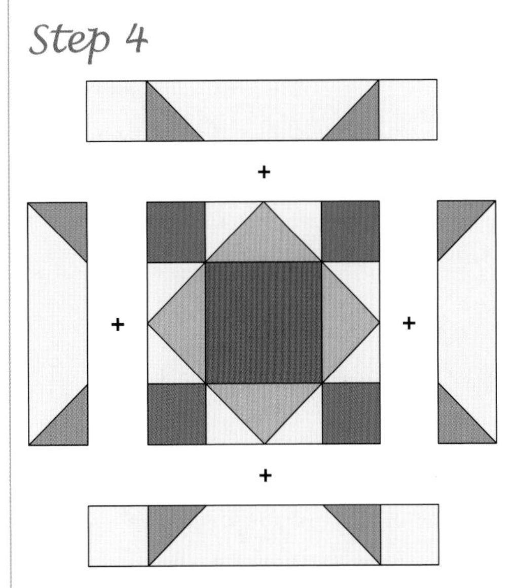

R Block

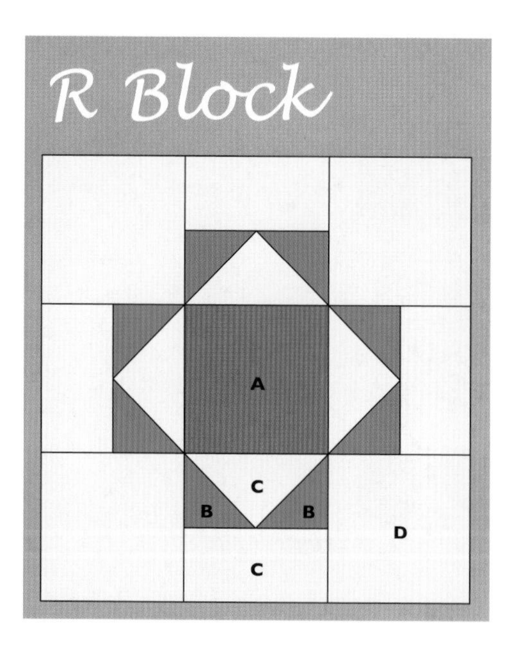

Cutting Instructions

PIECE	COLOR	# PIECES	CUT SIZE
A		1	3½″ × 3½″
B		8	2″ × 2″
C		8	2″ × 3½″
D		4	3½″ × 3½″

Piecing Instructions

Refer to page 74 for instructions for piecing the blocks using the techniques listed with the piecing diagrams below.

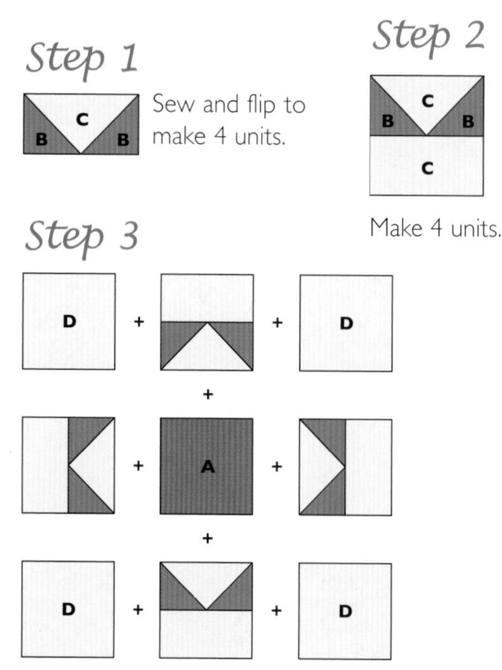

X4 Block

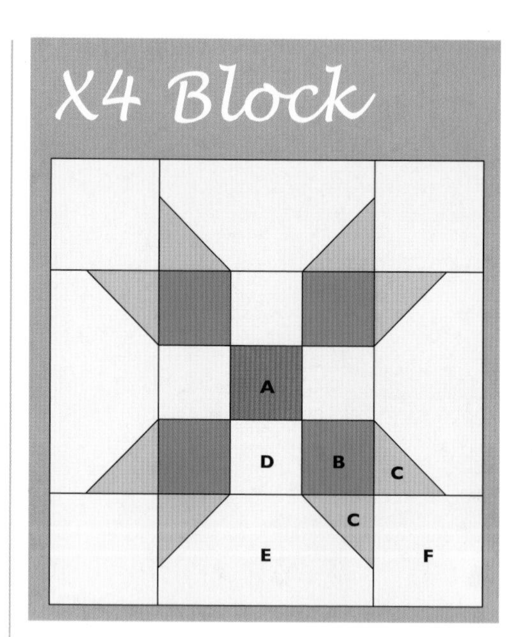

Cutting Instructions

PIECE	COLOR	# PIECES	CUT SIZE
A		1	2″ × 2″
B		4	2″ × 2″
C		8	2″ × 2″
D		4	2″ × 2″
E		4	2¾″ × 5″
F		4	2¾″ × 2¾″

Piecing Instructions

Refer to page 74 for instructions for piecing the blocks using the techniques listed with the piecing diagrams below.

Step 1

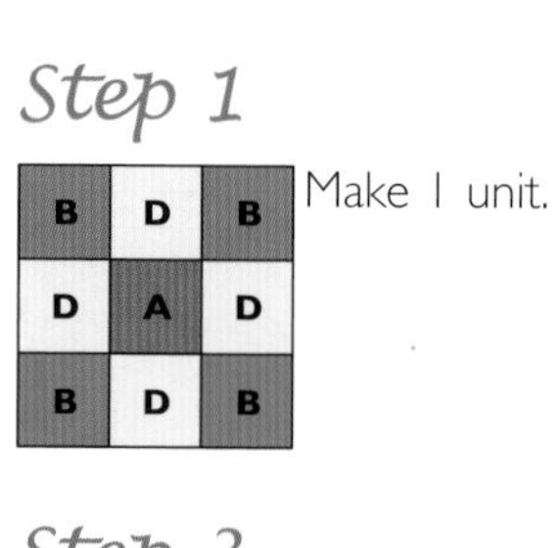

Make 1 unit.

Step 2

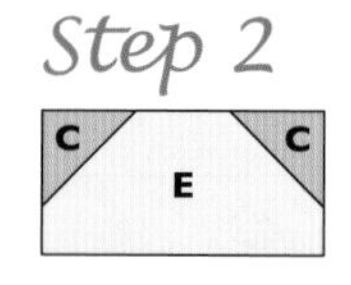

Sew and flip to make 4 units.

Step 3

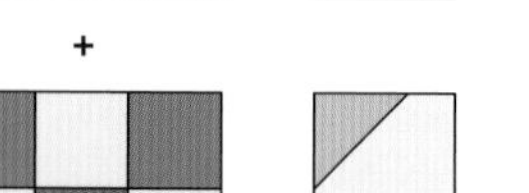

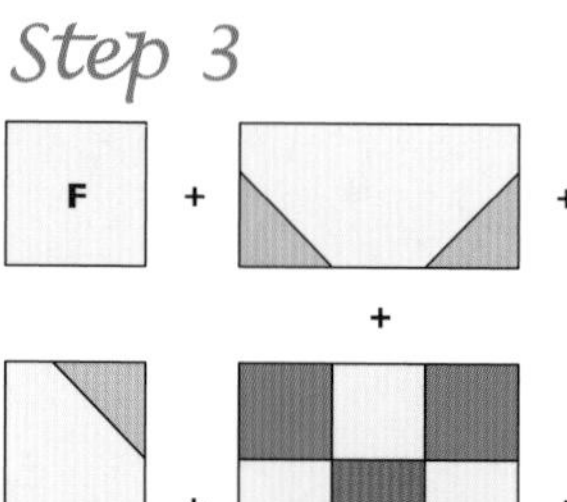

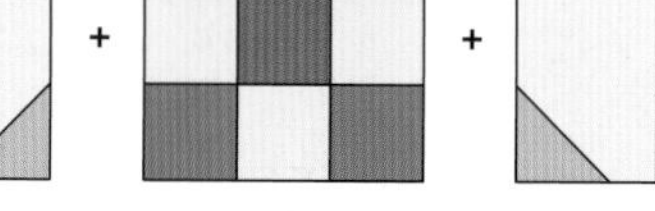

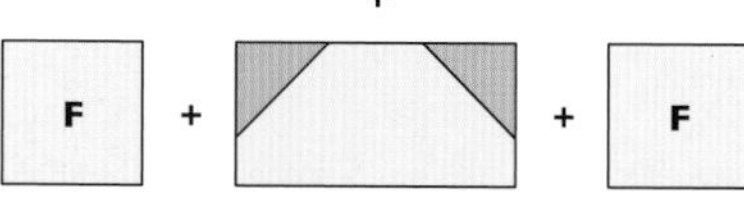

The Arrow Crown Quilts

Brite Bugs

FINISHED SIZE
53″ × 53″

FINISHED BLOCKS
12″

SETTING
Horizontal 3 × 3

BLOCKS USED
A, page 8
B1, page 9
L, page 14

Machine quilted by Jan Korytkowski

The bright primary colors and the "buggy" border fabric enliven this quilt's otherwise ordinary 3 × 3 horizontal set. With only nine blocks, there's not usually a lot of opportunity for exciting quilt design, but this quilt is energetic. The two backgrounds in the corners of the L blocks also give it a rakish, on-point look.

Materials

See Construction Guidelines, page 74.

FABRIC	YARDAGE	USED FOR	NUMBER OF PIECES	CUT SIZE
PRINT	2 yards	Block A, piece A	1	3½″ × 3½″
		Block B1, piece A	4	3½″ × 3½″
		Block L, piece E	4	3½″ × 5″
		Block L, piece F	4	5″ × 8″
		Block L, piece G	8	2″ × 3½″
		Block L, piece H	4	2⅜″ × 2⅜″
		Second border	8	Template B (page 76)
			4	Template E (page 77)
			4	Template E reversed (page 77)
		Third border	6	4″ × fabric width
PURPLE	¾ yard	Block A, piece C	8	2″ × 2″
		Block A, piece D	4	2″ × 3½″
		First border	4	2″ × 40½″
		Binding	6	2¼″ × fabric width
GOLD	⅜ yard	Block A, piece E	4	2″ × 2″
		Block A, piece F	4	2⅜″ × 2⅜″
		Block B1, piece D	16	2″ × 2″
		Block B1, piece E	16	2⅜″ × 2⅜″
BLUE	⅓ yard	Block A, piece G	16	2″ × 2″
		Block A, piece H	4	2⅜″ × 2⅜″
		First border corner squares	4	2″ × 2″
		Second border corner squares	4	4″ × 4″
RED	⅜ yard	Block A, piece B	12	2″ × 2″
		Block B1, piece B	32	2″ × 2″
		Block B1, piece C	16	2″ × 3½″
		Block L, piece B	8	2″ × 2″
GREEN	1⅓ yards	Block A, piece I	4	2⅜″ × 2⅜″
		Block B1, piece F	16	2⅜″ × 2⅜″
		Block B1, piece G	64	2″ × 2″
		Block L, piece C	16	2″ × 2″
		Block L, piece D	8	2⅜″ × 2⅜″
		Second border	12	Template A (page 78)
PINK	⅔ yard	Block L, piece A	4	3½″ × 3½″
		Second border	12	Template C (page 78)
			12	Template D (page 76)

tip

The pieced second border adds a lot of interest to this otherwise simple quilt. Don't be intimidated by the sharp points—with a little preparation, the triangles are very easy to piece. Refer to the Construction Guidelines on page 74.

FABRIC	YARDAGE	USED FOR	NUMBER OF PIECES	CUT SIZE
CREAM	1¼ yards	Block A, piece J	8	2″ × 3½″
		Block A, piece K	4	2⅜″ × 2⅜″
		Block A, piece L	4	2″ × 2″
		Block B1, piece H	48	2″ × 3½″
		Block B1, piece I	16	2″ × 2″
		Block B1, piece J	16	2″ × 5″
		Block L, piece E	4	3½″ × 5″
		Block L, piece F	4	5″ × 8″
		Block L, piece G	8	2 × 3½″
		Block L, piece H	4	2⅜″ × 2⅜″
		Block L, piece I	16	2″ × 2″
BACKING	3½ yards			
BATTING	60″ × 60″			

Construction

Read through these instructions and the Construction Guidelines on page 74 for cutting and piecing techniques before beginning your quilt.

Refer to the Quilt Assembly Diagram and sew the blocks into horizontal rows. Press seams on odd rows to the left and even rows to the right. Sew together rows of blocks to complete the quilt top.

Borders

Add the borders one at a time, pressing toward the last border added. Using the Assembly Diagram as a guide for the second border, piece four border strips of three green triangles each. Refer to the Assembly Diagram for the sewing sequence. See page 75 for tips on piecing diamonds and triangles. Template patterns are on pages 76–78.

Blocks

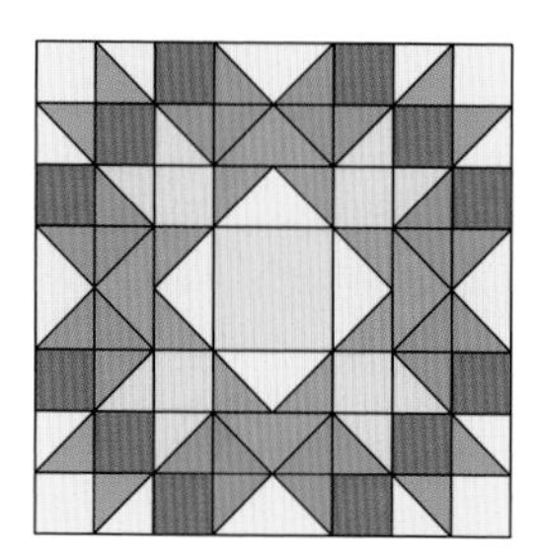

Block A, make 1. Instructions on page 8.

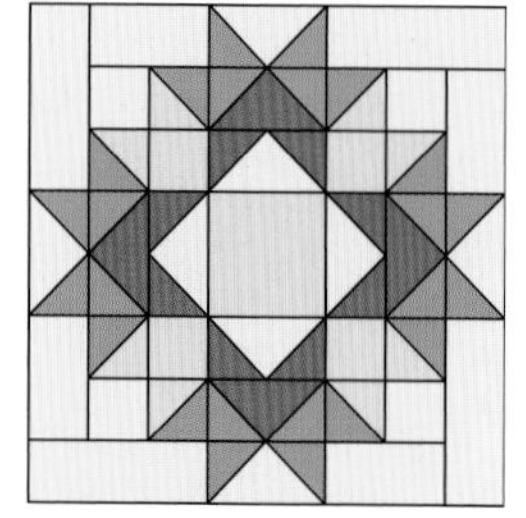

Block B1, make 4 identical. Instructions on page 9.

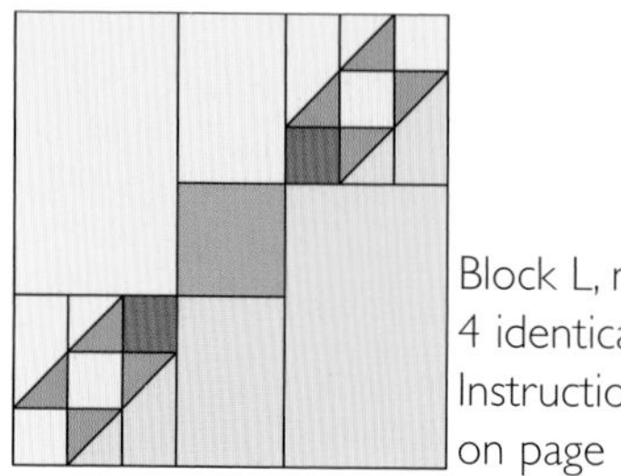

Block L, make 4 identical. Instructions on page 14.

Finishing

Prepare the backing (see page 75).

Layer and pin or baste the quilt top, batting, and backing. Quilt as desired.

Prepare binding (see page 75), and bind the quilt.

Assembly Diagram

More Design Options

Each of these alternate designs uses a horizontal 3 × 3 setting.

8 × 8 grid blocks: A, D, L

8 × 8 grid blocks: A, C1, C2

6 x 6 grid blocks: M, R, X4

6 x 6 grid blocks: N1, S, X3

6 x 6 grid blocks: Q, X4

6 x 6 grid blocks: L3, N1, X3

6 x 6 grid blocks: A1, N1, P

8 x 8 grid blocks: E1, L1, X2

8 x 8 grid blocks: A, C, L

Autumn Richness

FINISHED SIZE
59½″ × 59½″

FINISHED BLOCKS
9″

SETTING
Horizontal 4 × 4

BLOCKS USED
I, page 19
L3, page 22

Machine quilted by Lyla Pack

Although this quilt uses only two blocks, the three different sashing colors and the pieced diamond border make it really vibrant. The diagonal motion created by the L3 blocks paired with the diamonds in the border creates a lot more movement than you would expect from a straight set.

Materials

See Construction Guidelines, page 74.

FABRIC	YARDAGE	USED FOR	NUMBER OF PIECES	CUT SIZE
GREEN	1¼ yards	Block I, piece A	8	3½″ × 3½″
		Block L3, piece A	8	3½″ × 3½″
		Sashing	12	2″ × 9½″
		Second border	12	Template A (page 78)
BLACK PRINT	2 yards	Block I, piece B	32	2″ × 3½″
		Sashing	8	2″ × 9½″
		First border	5	2″ × fabric width
		Third border	6	5″ × fabric width
		Binding	6	2¼″ × fabric width
RUST	⅔ yard	Block I, piece D	32	2⅜″ × 2⅜″
		Block L3, piece C	16	2⅜″ × 2⅜″
		Block I, piece E	32	2″ × 2″
		Block L3, piece B	16	2″ × 2″
		Sashing squares	9	2″ × 2″
		First border corner squares	4	2″ × 2″
		Second border corner squares	4	4″ × 4″
		Third border corner squares	4	5″ × 5″
BROWN	½ yard	Block I, piece C	32	2″ × 3½″
		Block I, piece F	16	2″× 2″
		Block L3, piece E	16	2″× 2″
GOLD	2½ yards	Block I, piece F	144	2″ × 2″
		Block I, piece G	32	2⅜″ × 2⅜″
		Block L3, piece D	16	2⅜″ × 2⅜″
		Block L3, piece F	16	3½″ × 3½″
		Block L3, piece G	16	3½″ × 6½″
		Sashing	4	2″ × 9½″
		Second border	24	Template B (page 78)
		Second border	24	Template B reversed (page 78)
BACKING	3¾ yards			
BATTING	66″ × 66″			

tip

To perk up a horizontal setting, use a diagonal block (like one of the L blocks) to create interest. Change the sashing color around the center four blocks to add sparkle to this quilt.

Construction

Read through these instructions and the Construction Guidelines on page 74 for cutting and piecing techniques before beginning your quilt.

Blocks

Block I, make 8 identical blocks. Instructions on page 19.

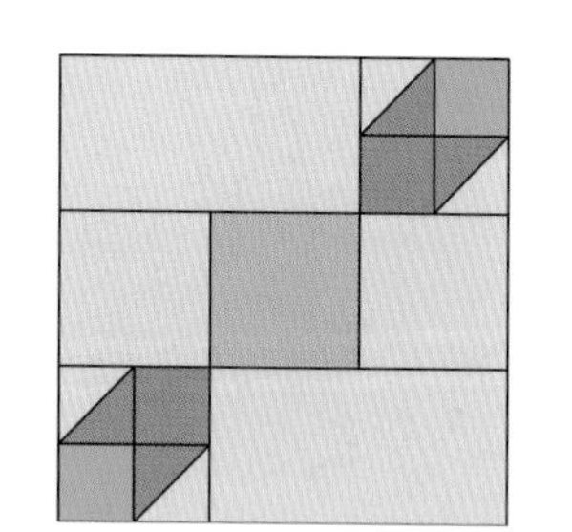

Block L3, make 8 identical blocks. Instructions on page 22.

Refer to the Assembly Diagram to sew the blocks and sashings into horizontal rows. Press seams on odd rows to the left and even rows to the right. Sew together rows of blocks and sashing strips to complete the quilt top.

Assembly Diagram

Borders

Add the borders one at a time, pressing toward the last border added.

Use the Border Assembly Diagram for the second border, to sew four gold triangles to each green diamond. Piece four border strips of three diamond units each. See page 75 for tips on piecing diamonds and triangles. Template patterns are on page 78.

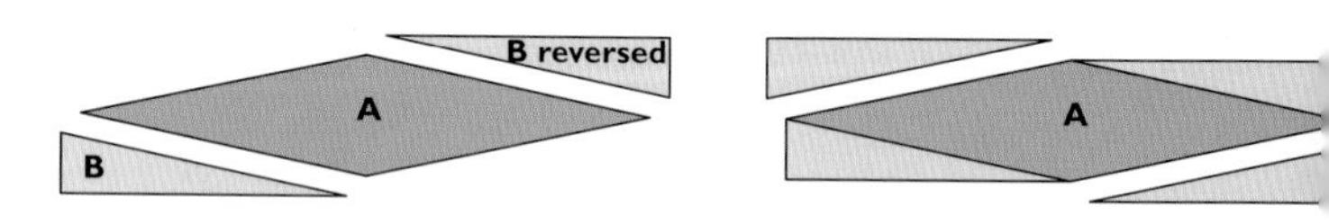

Border Assembly Diagram

Finishing

Prepare the backing (see page 75).

Layer and pin or baste the quilt top, batting, and backing. Quilt as desired.

Prepare the binding (see page 75), and bind the quilt.

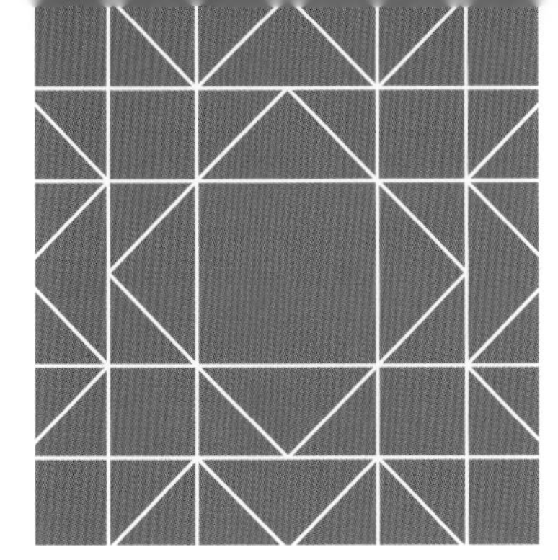

More Design Options

Each of these alternate designs uses a horizontal 4 × 4 setting.

6 × 6 grid blocks: A1, M

8 × 8 grid blocks: C, C2, L1

8 × 8 grid blocks: L, L1

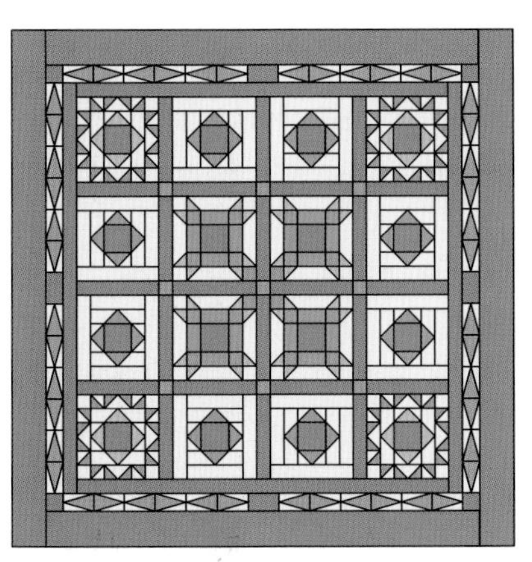

6 × 6 grid blocks: N1, P, S

8 × 8 grid blocks: L2

6 × 6 grid blocks: A1, M, X4

8 × 8 grid blocks: B, X1

8 × 8 grid blocks: B, L

6 × 6 grid blocks: A1, M

Memories from the Mills

FINISHED SIZE
85″ × 85″

FINISHED BLOCKS
12″

SETTING
Horizontal 5 × 5

BLOCKS USED
A, page 8
C1, page 10
L, page 14
X, page 15

Machine quilted by Jan Korytkowski

This quilt is a great showcase for the From the Mills reproduction fabric collections. It gets its punch from the bands of blue fabric between the rows of L and X blocks and the repeating blue in the pieced second border. The L and X blocks in this quilt are very simple and quick to piece. They make even big quilts doable for today's busy quilters.

Materials

See Construction Guidelines, page 74.

FABRIC	YARDAGE	USED FOR	NUMBER OF PIECES	CUT SIZE
DARK PRINT	4¾ yards	Block A, piece A	5	3½″ × 3½″
		Block A, piece B	60	2″ × 2″
		Block C1, piece A	4	3½″ × 3½″
		Block L, piece A	12	3½″ × 3½″
		Block X, piece A	4	3½″ × 3½″
		First border	7	3½″ × fabric width
		Second border	12	Template B (page 76-77)
			12	Template B reversed (page 76-77)
		Third border	8	5½″ × fabric width
		Binding	10	2¼″ × fabric width
RED	½ yard	Block A, piece E	20	2″ × 2″
		Block A, piece F	20	2⅜″ × 2⅜″
		Block L, piece B	24	2″ × 2″
		Block X, piece B	16	2″ × 2″
GREEN	1¼ yards	Block A, piece G	80	2″ × 2″
		Block A, piece H	20	2⅜″ × 2⅜″
		Block C1, piece D	96	2″ × 2″
		Block L, piece C	48	2″ × 2″
		Block L, piece D	24	2⅜″ × 2⅜″
		Block X, piece C	16	2⅜″ × 2⅜″
		Block X, piece D	32	2″ × 2″
PINK	¼ yard	Block A, piece I	20	2⅜″ × 2⅜″
BLUE	3½ yards	Block A, piece C	40	2″ × 2″
		Block A, piece D	20	2″ × 3½″
		Block C1, piece B	32	2″ × 2″
		Block C1, piece C	16	2″ × 3½″
		Block L, piece E	12	3½″ × 5″
		Block L, piece F	12	5″ × 8″
		Block L, piece G	24	2″ × 3½″
		Block L, piece H	12	2⅜″ × 2⅜″
		Block X, piece F	8	2⅜″ × 2⅜″
		Block X, piece G	16	2″ × 3½″
		Block X, piece H	8	3½″ × 5″
		First border corner squares	4	3½″ × 3½″
		Second border corner squares	4	5″ × 5″

tip

Double rows of L blocks help break up the wide expanse of background fabric and provide open space for fancy quilting and/or appliqué.

FABRIC	YARDAGE	USED FOR	NUMBER OF PIECES	CUT SIZE
BLUE CONTINUED		Second border	12	Template A (page 76–77)
		Third border corner square	4	5½″ × 5½″
CREAM	2½ yards	Block A, piece J	40	2″ × 3½″
		Block A, piece K	20	2⅜″ × 2⅜″
		Block A, piece L	20	2″ × 2″
		Block C1, piece E	48	2″ × 3½″
		Block C1, piece F	16	3½″ × 3½″
		Block C1, piece G	16	2″ × 5″
		Block L, piece E	12	3½″ × 5″
		Block L, piece F	12	5″ × 8″
		Block L, piece G	24	2″ × 3½″
		Block L, piece H	12	2⅜″ × 2⅜″
		Block L, piece I	48	2″ × 2″
		Block X, piece E	32	2″ × 2″
		Block X, piece F	8	2⅜″ × 2⅜″
		Block X, piece G	16	2″ × 3½″
		Block X, piece H	8	3½″ × 5″
Backing	7¾ yards			
Batting	90″ × 90″			

Construction

Read through these instructions and the Construction Guidelines on page 74 for cutting and piecing techniques before beginning your quilt.

Blocks

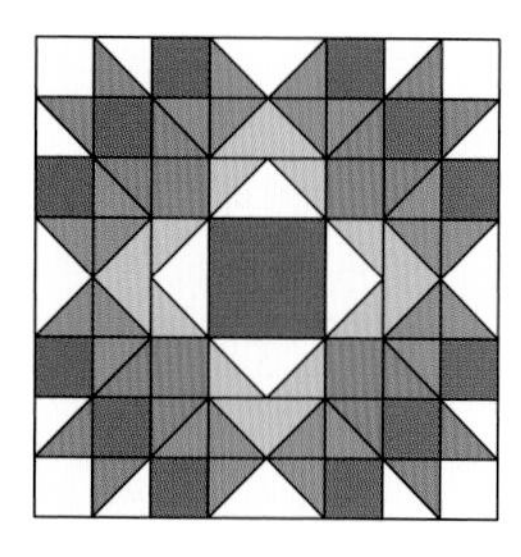

Block A, make 5 identical. Instructions on page 8.

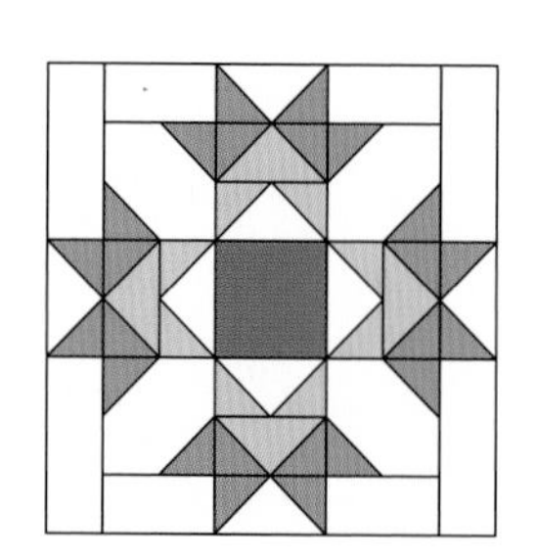

Block C1, make 4 identical. Instructions on page 10.

Block L, make 12 identical. Instructions on page 14.

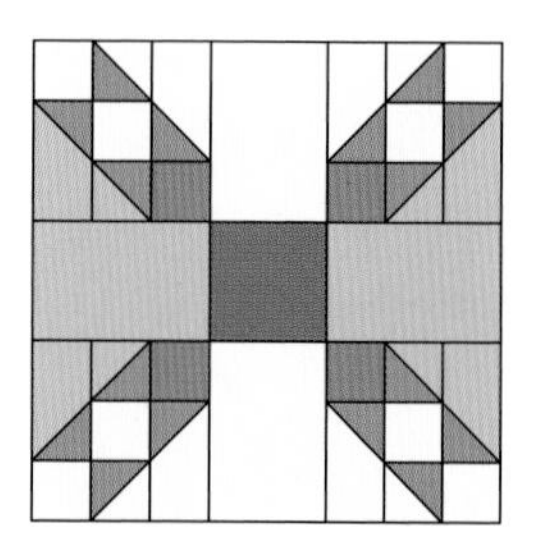

Block X, make 4 identical. Instructions on page 15.

Refer to the Assembly Diagram to sew the blocks into horizontal rows. Press seams on odd rows to the left and even rows to the right. Sew together rows of blocks to complete the quilt top.

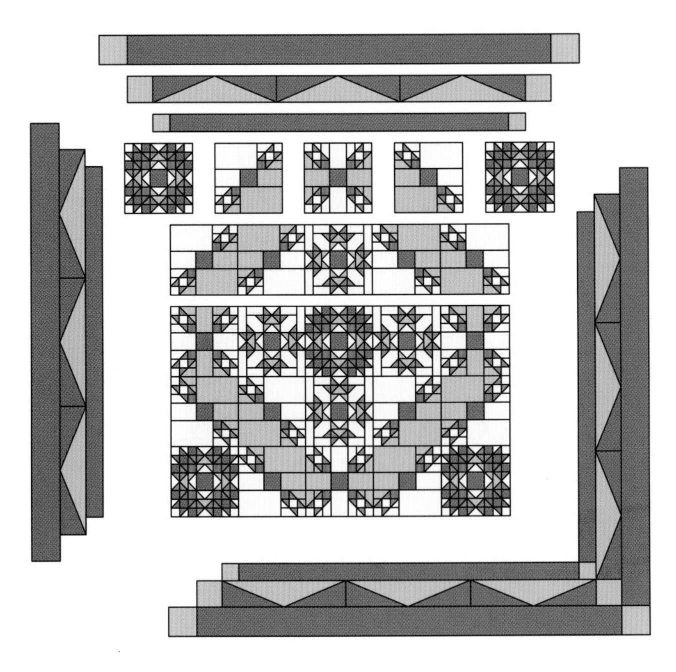

Assembly Diagram

Borders

Add the borders one at a time, pressing toward the last border added. Use the Assembly Diagram for the second border, and piece two dark print triangles to each blue triangle. Piece four border strips of three blue diamond units each. See page 75 for tips on piecing diamonds and triangles. Template patterns are on page 76–77.

Finishing

Prepare the backing (see page 75).

Layer and pin or baste the quilt top, batting, and backing. Quilt as desired.

Prepare the binding (see page 75), and bind the quilt.

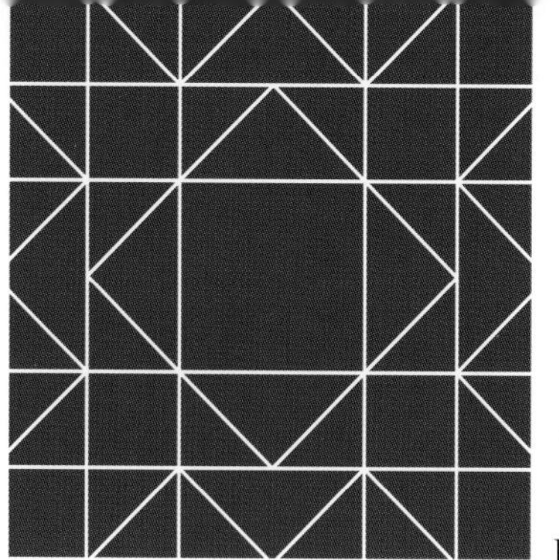

More Design Options

Each of these alternate designs uses a horizontal 5 × 5 setting.

8 × 8 grid blocks: A, C1, C2

6 × 6 grid blocks: I, L4, O, S

8 × 8 grid blocks: C, F, G, L, X

6 × 6 grid blocks: I, L3, S

8 × 8 grid blocks: A, C1, F, L

6 × 6 grid blocks: H1, L3, R, S

8 × 8 grid blocks: A, B1, G, L, X

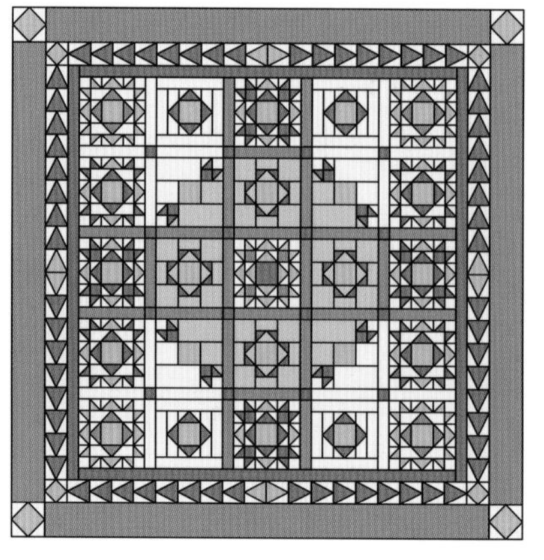

6 × 6 grid blocks: I, L3, N, R, S

8 × 8 grid blocks: A, C, G, L2

Dark Treasures

Machine quilted by Wanda Jones

Nothing brings out and intensifies color and detail like a black background. The circular motion of the blocks and the quilting pop out from the dark background. The colored rectangles in the first and third borders stand out and add to the simple charm of this quilt. Mixing several prints in each color family makes a happy, scrappy quilt.

FINISHED SIZE
57″ × 75″

FINISHED BLOCKS
9″

SETTING
Horizontal 5 × 7

BLOCKS USED
I, page 19
L4, page 23
N, page 24
X4, page 26

Materials

See Construction Guidelines, page 74.

FABRIC	YARDAGE	USED FOR	NUMBER OF PIECES	CUT SIZE
PURPLE	1 yard	Block I, piece A	7	3½″ × 3½″
		Block N, piece D	48	2⅜″ × 2⅜″
		Block X4, piece C	32	2″ × 2″
		First border	15	2″ × 4″
			3	2″ × 2¼″
		Third border	7	3½″ × 7½″
PINK	1 yard	Block I, piece C	28	2″ × 3½″
		Block N, piece A	12	3½″ × 3½″
		Block X4, piece A	4	2″ × 2″
		First border	11	2″ × 4″
			2	2″ × 2¼″
		Third border	7	3½″ × 7½″
			8	3½″ × 5½″
BLUE	1¼ yards	Block I, piece B	28	2″ × 3½″
		Block N, piece C	48	2″ × 3½″
		Block L4, piece B	24	2″ × 2″
		First border	14	2″ × 4″
		First border corner squares	4	2″ × 2″
		Third border	8	3½″ × 7½″
		Third border corner squares	4	3½″ × 3½″
GREEN	1⅓ yards	Block I, piece D	28	2⅜″ × 2⅜″
		Block I, piece E	28	2″ × 2″
		Block N, piece B	48	2″ × 3½″
		Block L4, piece C	48	2″ × 2″
		Block X4, piece B	16	2″ × 2″
		First border	18	2″ × 4″
			3	2″ × 2¼″
		Third border	6	3½″ × 7½″
YELLOW	¼ yard	Block L4, piece A	12	2″ × 2″
BLACK	4½ yards	Block I, piece F	140	2″ × 2″
		Block I, piece G	28	2⅜″ × 2⅜″
		Block N, piece E	48	2″ × 3½″
		Block N, piece F	192	2″ × 2″

tip

Everyone's sewing is a little different. This quilt's pieced borders are especially forgiving, so it's a great starter for quilters who haven't worked with pieced borders before. When piecing these borders, leave the end pieces a little long, then measure the quilt top and trim the opposite borders to equal lengths to square up the quilt. Add corner pieces to the ends of the long borders, then add the borders to the quilt.

FABRIC	YARDAGE	USED FOR	NUMBER OF PIECES	CUT SIZE
BLACK CONTINUED		Block N, piece G	48	2⅜″ × 2⅜″
		Block L4, piece D	24	2″ × 2″
		Block L4, piece E	24	2″ × 3½″
		Block L4, piece F	24	2¾″ × 5″
		Block L4, piece G	24	2¾″ × 7¼″
		Block L4, piece H	24	2¾″ × 2¾″
		Block X4, piece D	16	2″ × 2″
		Block X4, piece E	16	2¾″ × 5″
		Block X4, piece F	16	2¾″ × 2¾″
		Second border	7	2″ × fabric width
		Binding	7	2¼″ × fabric width
BACKING	4¾ yards			
BATTING	63″ × 81″			

Construction

Read through these instructions and the Construction Guidelines on page 74 for cutting and piecing techniques before beginning your quilt.

Blocks

Refer to the Assembly Diagram to sew the blocks into horizontal rows. Press seams on odd rows to the left and even rows to the right. Sew together rows of blocks to complete the quilt top.

Borders

Add the borders one at a time, pressing toward the last border added. For the first and third borders, piece as shown in the Assembly Diagram. Measure the quilt top and cut the borders to fit. Make any adjustments, then add the corner squares.

Finishing

Prepare the backing (see page 75).

Layer and pin or baste the quilt top, batting, and backing. Quilt as desired.

Prepare binding (see page 75), and finish the quilt.

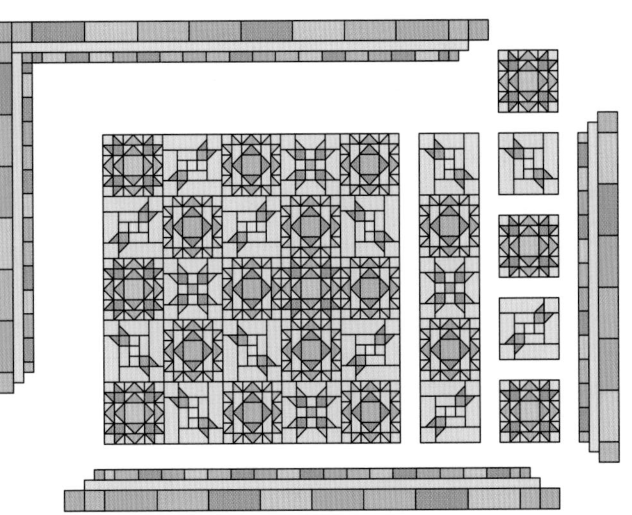

Assembly Diagram

Block I, make 7 identical. Instructions on page 19.

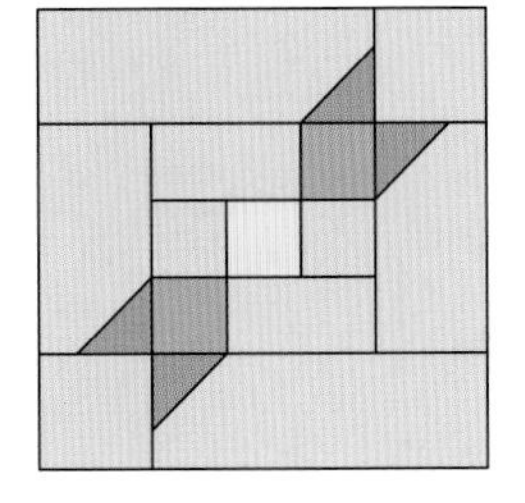

Block L4, make 12 identical. Instructions on page 23.

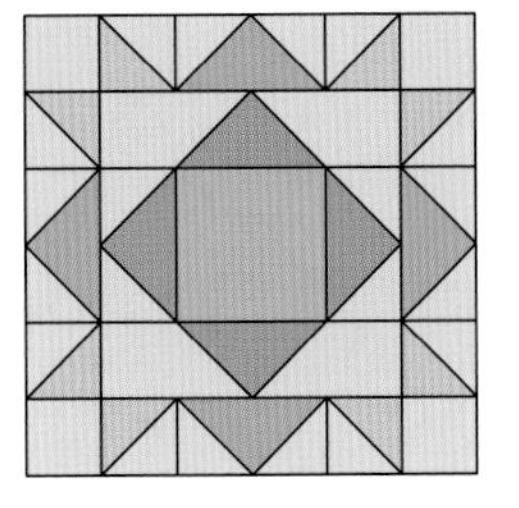

Block N, make 12 identical. Instructions on page 24.

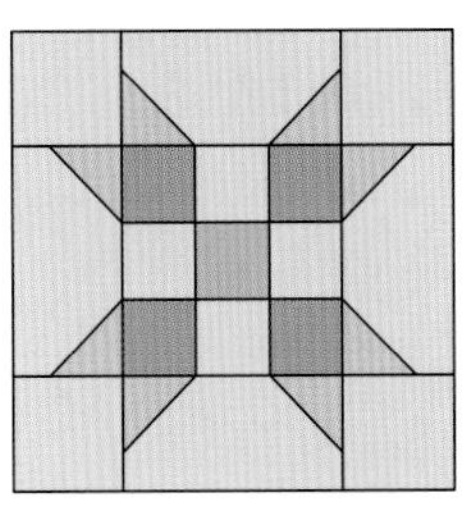

Block X4, make 4 identical. Instructions on page 26.

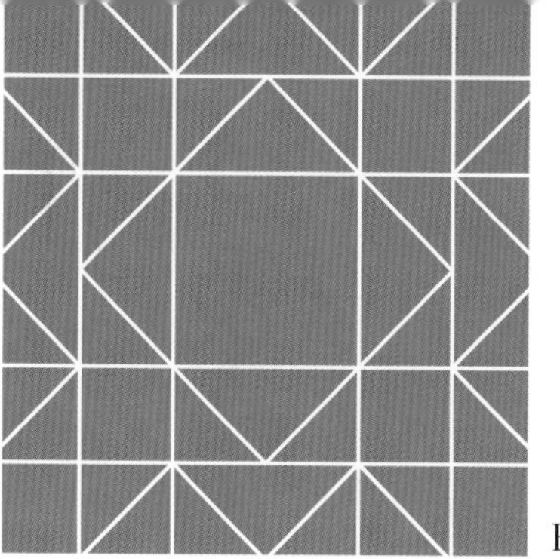

More Design Options

Each of these alternate designs uses a horizontal 5 × 7 setting.

6 × 6 grid blocks: H1, L4, N, R, S, X4

6 × 6 grid blocks: I, L3, L4, S, X3, X4

8 × 8 grid blocks: A, C, E1, F, G

6 × 6 grid blocks: H1, J, L4, S

6 × 6 grid blocks: A1, H, N1, L4, R, X4

8 × 8 grid blocks: A, D, E1, L, X

8 × 8 grid blocks: B1, C2, F, X1

8 × 8 grid blocks: A, D, E1, L, X

8 × 8 grid blocks: A, F, L, L2, X, X2

Indonesian Splendor

Machine quilted by Wanda Jones

Jazzed-up sashing strips and setting triangles enliven this simple 3 × 3 on-point quilt setting. The sashing alternates between background and print fabrics, either blending with or setting off the blocks. The G blocks float outside the sashing frame, along with setting triangles made of half- and quarter-blocks that echo the inner F blocks. The overall effect expands the visual quilt surface.

FINISHED SIZE
68½″ × 68½″

FINISHED BLOCKS
12″

SETTING
On-Point 3 × 3

BLOCKS USED

B1, page 9
E1, page 11
F, page 12
F half, page 48
F quarter, page 48
G, page 13

Materials

See Construction Guidelines, page 74.

FABRIC	YARDAGE	USED FOR	NUMBER OF PIECES	CUT SIZE
RED	2 yards	Block B1, piece A	1	3½″ × 3½″
		Block F, piece A	4	3½″ × 3½″
		Block G, piece A	4	3½″ × 3½″
		Block ½ F, piece A	8	3½″ × 3½″
		Block ¼ F, piece A	4	3½″ × 3½″
		Second border	7	4½″ × fabric width
		Binding	8	2¼″ × fabric width
LIGHT BLUE	1 yard	Block B1, piece B	8	2″ × 2″
		Block B1, piece C	4	2″ × 3½″
		Block ½ F, piece B	16	2″ × 3½″
		Block ¼ F, piece B	4	2″ × 3½″
		Block G, piece B	16	2″ × 3½″
		Sashing	16	2″ × 12½″
		First border corner squares	4	2″ × 2″
DARK BLUE	⅔ yard	Block B1, piece D	4	2″ × 2″
		Block B1, piece E	4	2⅜″ × 2⅜″
		Block E1, piece A	16	2″ × 3½″
		Block F, piece C	16	2″ × 2″
		Block ½ F, piece C	56	2″ × 2″
		Block ¼ F, piece C	16	2″ × 2″
GREEN	¾ yard	Block B1, piece F	4	2⅜″ × 2⅜″
		Block B1, piece G	16	2″ × 2″
		Block E1, piece C	16	2″ × 2″
		Block E1, piece D	16	2⅜″ × 2⅜″
		Block F, piece B	16	2″ × 3½″
		Sashing squares	16	2″ × 2″
		Second border corner squares	4	4½″ × 4½″
BROWN	1 yard	Block E1, piece B	16	2″ × 3½″
		Block F, piece C	32	2″ × 2″
		Block G, piece C	32	2″ × 2″
		Block G, piece D	16	2⅜″ × 2⅜″
		First border	6	2″ × fabric width

tip

Piece the side and corner setting triangles using full squares on the outside edges, then trim them after piecing. (Be sure to include ¼″ seam allowances.) You cannot simply make a full block and cut it in half or in fourths, because you would have no seam allowance on the cut edge.

FABRIC	YARDAGE	USED FOR	NUMBER OF PIECES	CUT SIZE
TAN	3½ yards	Block B1, piece H	12	2″ × 3½″
		Block B1, piece I	4	2″ × 2″
		Block B1, piece J	4	2″ × 5″
		Block E1, piece E	48	2″ × 2″
		Block E1, piece F	16	2⅜″ × 2⅜″
		Block E1, piece G	8	2″ × 9½″
		Block E1, piece H	8	2″ × 12½″
		Block E1, piece I	4	3½″ × 3½″
		Block F, piece D	16	3½″ × 6½″
		Block F, piece E	32	2″ × 2″
		Block F, piece F	16	3½″ × 3½″
		Block ½ F, piece D	16	3½″ × 6½″
		Block ½ F, piece E	32	2″ × 2″
		Block ½ F, piece F	24	3½″ × 3½″
		Block ¼ F, piece D	4	3½″ × 6½″
		Block ¼ F, piece E	8	2″ × 2″
		Block ¼ F, piece F	8	3½″ × 3½″
		Block G, piece E	32	2″ × 3½″
		Block G, piece F	16	2⅜″ × 2⅜″
		Block G, piece G	32	2″ × 2″
		Block G, piece H	8	2″ × 9½″
		Block G, piece I	8	2 × 12½″
		Sashing	20	2″ × 12½″
		Sashing squares	8	2″ × 2″
Backing	4½ yards			
Batting	74″ × 74″			

Construction

Read through these instructions and the Construction Guidelines on page 74 for cutting and piecing techniques before beginning your quilt.

Blocks

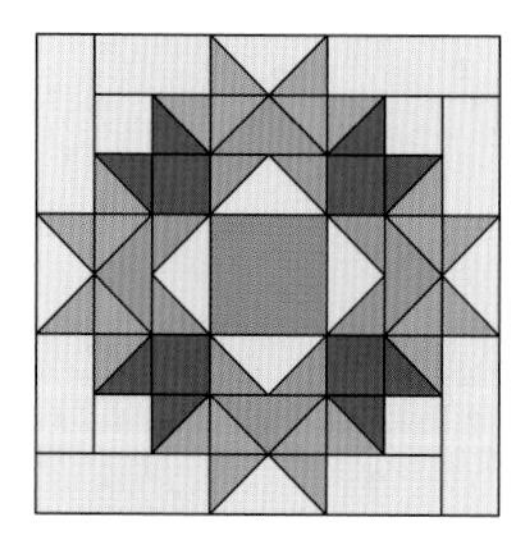

Block BI, make 1. Instructions on page 9.

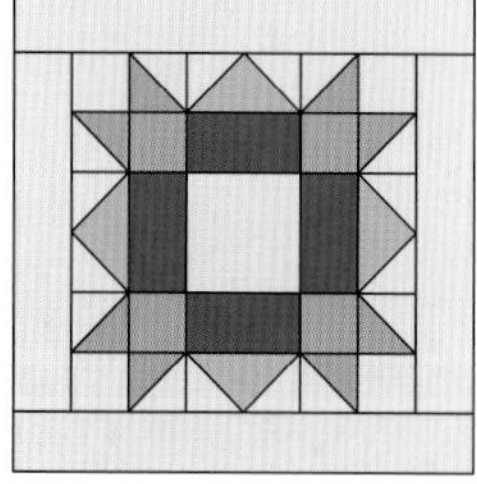

Block EI, make 4 identical. Instructions on page 11.

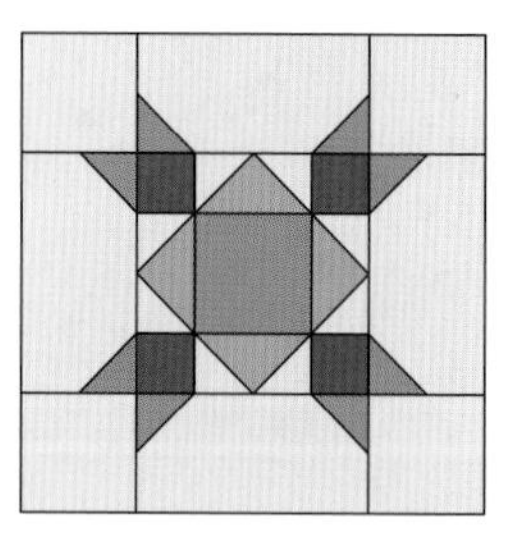

Block F, make 4 identical. Instructions on page 12.

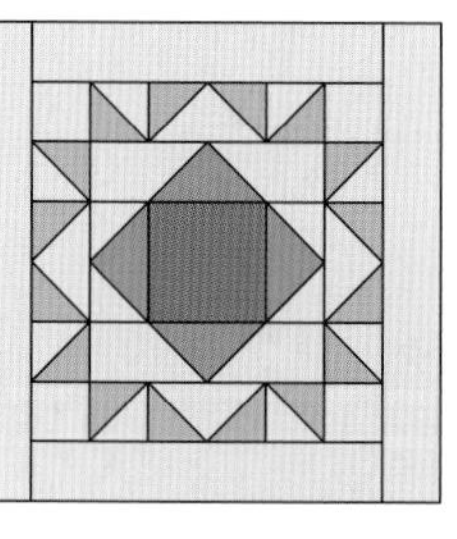

Block G, make 4 identical. Instructions on page 13.

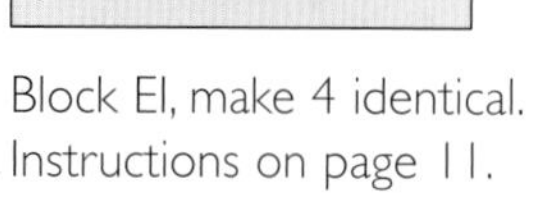

Block F half-block, make 8. Instructions on page 75.

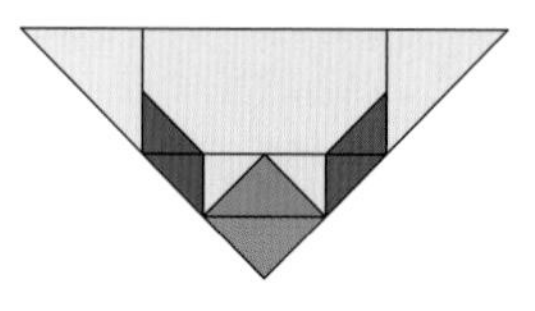

Block F quarter-block, make 4. Instructions on page 75.

Refer to the Assembly Diagram to sew the blocks and sashings into diagonal rows. Press seams on odd rows to the left and even rows to the right. Sew together rows of blocks and sashing strips to complete the quilt top. Add corner triangles after all rows are sewn together.

Assembly Diagram

Borders

Add the borders one at a time, pressing toward the last border added.

Finishing

Prepare the backing (see page 75).

Layer and pin or baste the quilt top, batting, and backing. Quilt as desired.

Prepare the binding (see page 75), and bind the quilt.

More Design Options

Each of these alternate designs uses an on-point 3 × 3 setting.

6 × 6 grid blocks: H1, O, S

8 × 8 grid blocks: A, B1, F, L1

6 × 6 grid blocks: K, M, Q, X4

8 × 8 grid blocks: A, D, E, L1

6 × 6 grid blocks: I, Q, R, X4

8 × 8 grid blocks: C, F, L1

6 × 6 grid blocks: K, P, R, X3

6 × 6 grid blocks: H, L3, N1, O

8 × 8 grid blocks: B, C1, E, G

Pastel Dreams

FINISHED SIZE
69″ × 86″

FINISHED BLOCKS
12″

SETTING
On-Point 3 × 4

BLOCKS USED
A, page 8
G, page 13
L, page 14
X, page 15

Machine quilted by Lyla Pack

Using two different background colors in both the L and X blocks (and careful planning) creates a wide pink "inner border" that fools the eye into thinking this is a horizontal-set quilt. I like to call this a controlled scrap quilt because it lends itself to using several fabrics from each color family.

Materials

See Construction Guidelines, page 74.

FABRIC	YARDAGE	USED FOR	NUMBER OF PIECES	CUT SIZE
YELLOW	½ yard	Block A, piece A	4	3½″ × 3½″
		Block A, piece L	4	2″ × 2″
		Block G, piece A	4	3½″ × 3½″
		Block L, piece A	6	3½″ × 3½″
		Block X, piece A	4	3½″ × 3½″
		First border corner squares	4	2″ × 2″
PINK	⅔ yard	Block A, piece B	48	2″ × 2″
		Block A, piece C	32	2″ × 2″
		Block A, piece D	16	2″ × 3½″
		Block G, piece B	16	2″ × 3½″
PINK DOT	2⅓ yards	Block L, piece B	12	2″ × 2″
		Block L, piece E	6	3½″ × 5″
		Block L, piece F	6	5″ × 8″
		Block L, piece G	12	2″ × 3½″
		Block L, piece H	6	2⅜″ × 2⅜″
		Block L, piece I	12	2″ × 2″
		Block X, piece B	16	2″ × 2″
		Block X, piece E	16	2″ × 2″
		Block X, piece F	12	2⅜″ × 2⅜″
		Block X, piece G	24	2″ × 3½″
		Block X, piece H	12	3½″ × 5″
		Setting triangles	3	18¼″ × 18¼″ (Cut twice diagonally for 10 side triangles.)
		Setting triangles	2	9½″ × 9½″ (Cut once diagonally for 4 corner triangles.)
GREEN	1 yard	Block A, piece G	64	2″ × 2″
		Block A, piece H	16	2⅜″ × 2⅜″
		Block G, piece C	32	2″ × 2″
		Block G, piece D	16	2⅜″ × 2⅜″
		Block L, piece C	24	2″ × 2″
		Block L, piece D	12	2⅜″ × 2⅜″
		Block X, piece C	16	2⅜″ × 2⅜″
		Block X, piece D	32	2″ × 2″

tip

In the A block, one corner square is a colored fabric instead of the background fabric. During construction, make sure all four of these contrasting corners come together at the center of the quilt. If the background fabric were at the center, the quilt would look much less compelling and more like it had a hole in the center.

FABRIC	YARDAGE	USED FOR	NUMBER OF PIECES	CUT SIZE
LAVENDER	2⅓ yards	Block A, piece E	16	2″ × 2″
		Block A, piece F	16	2⅜″ × 2⅜″
		Block A, piece I	16	2⅜″ × 2⅜″
		Block L, piece I	12	2″ × 2″
		Block X, piece E	16	2″ × 2″
		First border	7	2″ × fabric width
		Second border	84	2″ × 2″
			84	2⅜″ × 2⅜″
		Second border corner squares	4	3½″ × 3½″
		Third border corner squares	4	5″ × 5″
		Binding	9	2¼″ × fabric width
CREAM DOT	2⅓ yards	Block A, piece J	32	2″ × 3½″
		Block A, piece K	16	2⅜″ × 2⅜″
		Block A, piece L	12	2″ × 2″
		Block G, piece E	32	2″ × 3½″
		Block G, piece F	16	2⅜″ × 2⅜″
		Block G, piece G	32	2″ × 2″
		Block G, piece H	8	2″ × 9½″
		Block G, piece I	8	2″ × 12½″
		Block L, piece E	6	3½″ × 5″
		Block L, piece F	6	5″ × 8″
		Block L, piece G	12	2″ × 3½″
		Block L, piece H	6	2⅜″ × 2⅜″
		Block X, piece F	4	2⅜″ × 2⅜″
		Block X, piece G	8	2″ × 3½″
		Block X, piece H	4	3½″ × 5″
		Second border	84	2″ × 2″
			84	2⅜″ × 2⅜″
PRINT	1½ yards	Third border	8	5″ × fabric width
BACKING	5½ yards			
BATTING	75″ × 92″			

Construction

Read through these instructions and the Construction Guidelines on page 74 for cutting and piecing techniques before beginning your quilt.

Blocks

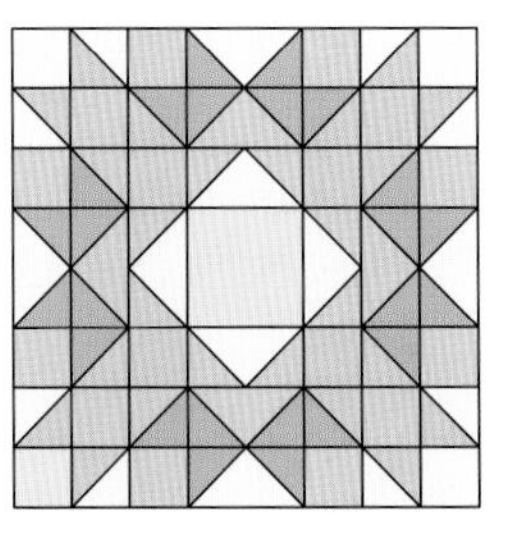

Block A, make 4 identical.
Instructions on page 8.

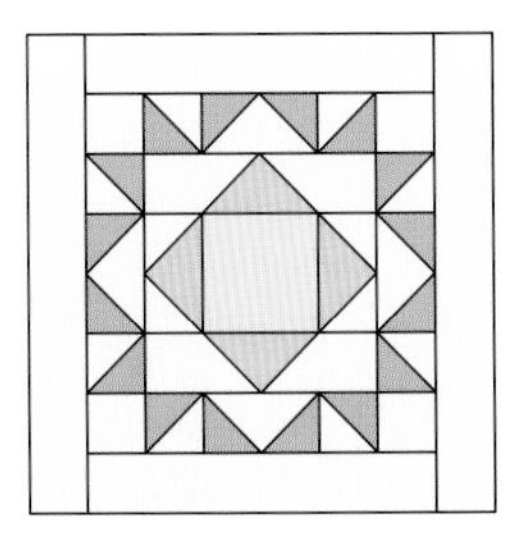

Block G, make 4 identical.
Instructions on page 13.

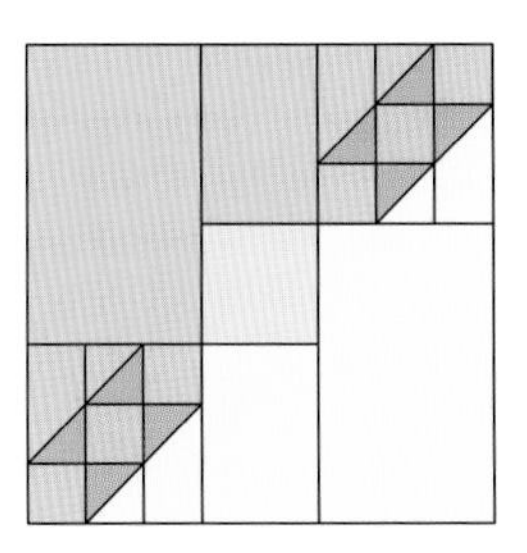

Block L, make 6 identical.
Instructions on page 14.

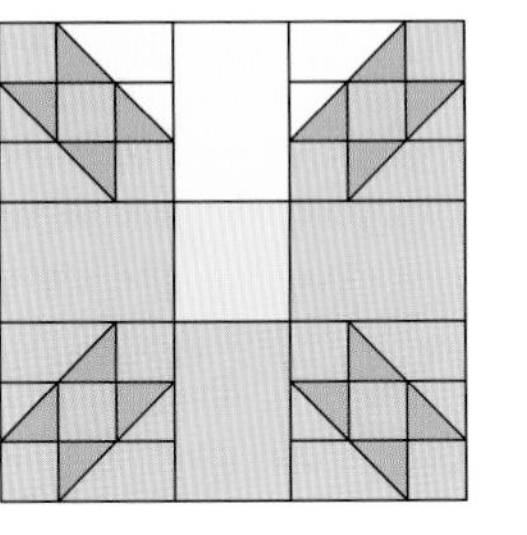

Block X, make 4 identical.
Instructions on page 15.

Refer to the Assembly Diagram to sew the blocks into diagonal rows. Press seams on odd rows to the left and even rows to the right. Sew together rows of blocks and side setting triangles to complete the quilt top. Add corner triangles after all rows are sewn together.

Assembly Diagram

Borders

Add the borders one at a time, pressing toward the last border added. For the second border, refer to the illustration below to make 42 border units from the lavender and the cream dot fabrics. Sew together nine units for each short side, and 12 units for each long side.

Border Unit
Make 42.

Finishing

Prepare the backing (see page 75).

Layer and pin or baste the quilt top, batting, and backing. Quilt as desired.

Prepare the binding (see page 75), and bind the quilt.

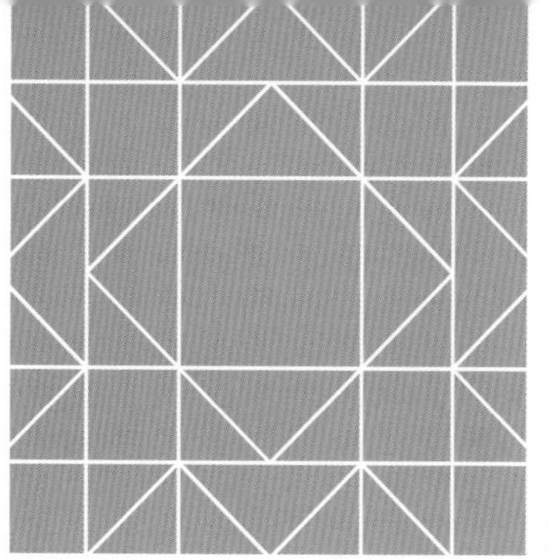

More Design Options

Each of these alternate designs uses an on-point 3 × 4 setting.

8 × 8 grid blocks: A, E, E1

6 × 6 grid blocks: K, L3, P, R, X3

6 × 6 grid blocks: L3, N, N1, X4

8 × 8 grid blocks: D, E, E1

8 × 8 grid blocks: B, B1, E1, F, ½F, ¼F

6 × 6 grid blocks: A1, I, L4, ½ X3, X4

8 × 8 grid blocks: B, B1, E1, F

8 × 8 grid blocks: B, B1, F, L, X

8 × 8 grid blocks: B, B1, F, ½ F, ¼ F, X

Leaf Colors

Machine quilted by Lyla Pack

FINISHED SIZE
62″ × 62″

FINISHED BLOCKS
9″

SETTING
On-Point 4 × 4

BLOCKS USED
A1, page 17
J, page 20
K, page 21
K half, page 57

The "sashing" in this quilt is actually an illusion—the A1 block has wide outer strips that form the green framing, and the J blocks are pieced with brown and green on opposite sides to give the effect of two on-point inner borders. Use the open spaces of the tan setting squares to show off your quilting skills.

Materials

See Construction Guidelines, page 74.

FABRIC	YARDAGE	USED FOR	NUMBER OF PIECES	CUT SIZE
DARK GREEN	1¼ yards	Block A1, piece E	7	2″ × 2″
		Block A1, piece G	7	3½″ × 6½″
		Block A1, piece H	7	3½″ × 9½″
		Block J, piece G	12	2″ × 9½″
		Block ½ K, piece G	8	2″ × 2″
		First border corner squares	4	2″ × 2″
		Second border corner squares	4	4½″ × 4½″
MEDIUM GREEN	½ yard	Block A1, piece A	7	2″ × 2″
		Block J, piece A	12	3½″ × 3½″
		Block K, piece A	4	3½″ × 3½″
		Block ½ K, piece A	4	3½″ × 3½″
LIGHT GREEN	1¼ yards	Block A1, piece F	14	2⅜″ × 2⅜″
		Block J, piece C	96	2″ × 2″
		Block K, piece C	32	2″ × 2″
		Block ½ K, piece C	16	2″ × 2″
		Setting triangles	2	14¼″ × 14¼″ (Cut twice diagonally for 8 side triangles.)
		Setting triangles	2	7⅜″ × 7⅜″ (Cut once diagonally for 4 corner triangles.)
TAN	¾ yard	Block A1, piece C	28	2″ × 2″
		Block A1, piece D	14	2⅜″ × 2⅜″
		Block J, piece G	12	2″ × 9½″
		Block K, piece D	16	2″ × 2″
		Block ½ K, piece D	12	2″ × 2″
		Block ½ K, piece F	4	2″ × 2″
BROWN	1⅜ yards	Block A1, piece B	21	2″ × 2″
		Block J, piece B	48	2″ × 2″
		Block K, piece B	32	2″ × 2″
		Block ½ K, piece B	16	2″ × 2″
		First border	6	2″ × fabric width
BINDING			7	2¼″ × fabric width

tip

Even if you aren't a color genius, you can make everyone think you are. Start your fabric selection with a focus print that has several colors and values. I started this quilt with the border print. Most multicolor print fabrics today have circles printed on the selvage that show each color used in the print. Use that "legend" as your guide as you pick coordinating solids and tone-on-tone fabrics.

FABRIC	YARDAGE	USED FOR	NUMBER OF PIECES	CUT SIZE
BEIGE	1¾ yards	Block A1, piece I	14	2″ × 3½″
		Block A1, piece J	14	2⅜″ × 2⅜″
		Block A1, piece K	7	2″ × 2″
		Block J, piece D	48	2″ × 3½″
		Block J, piece E	48	2″ × 2″
		Block J, piece F	24	2″ × 6½″
		Block K, piece E	48	2″ × 3½″
		Block K, piece F	16	2″ × 2″
		Block ½ K, piece E	16	2″ × 3½″
		Block ½ K, piece F	16	2″ × 2″
		Setting blocks	2	9½″ × 9½″
PRINT	1 yards	Second border	6	4½″ × fabric width
BACKING	3¾ yards			
BATTING	68″ × 68″			

Construction

Read through these instructions and the Construction Guidelines on page 74 for cutting and piecing techniques before beginning your quilt.

Blocks

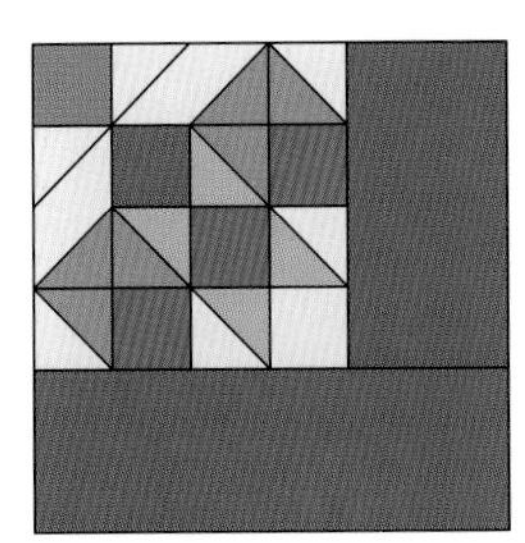

Block A1, make 7 identical. Instructions on page 17.

Block J, make 12 identical. Instructions on page 20.

Block K, make 4 identical. Instructions on page 21.

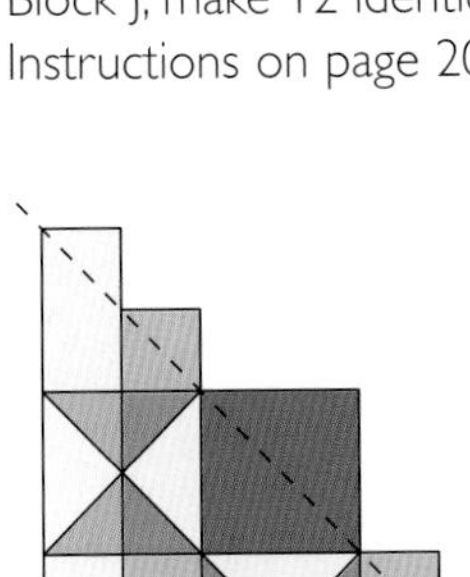

Block half-K, make 4 identical. Trim the diagonal edge, being sure to add ¼″ seam allowance. Instructions on page 75.

Refer to the Assembly Diagram to sew the blocks into diagonal rows. Press seams on odd rows to the left and even rows to the right. Sew together rows of blocks to complete the quilt top. Add corner triangles to row 4 after all rows are sewn together. For Borders and Finishing, see page 48.

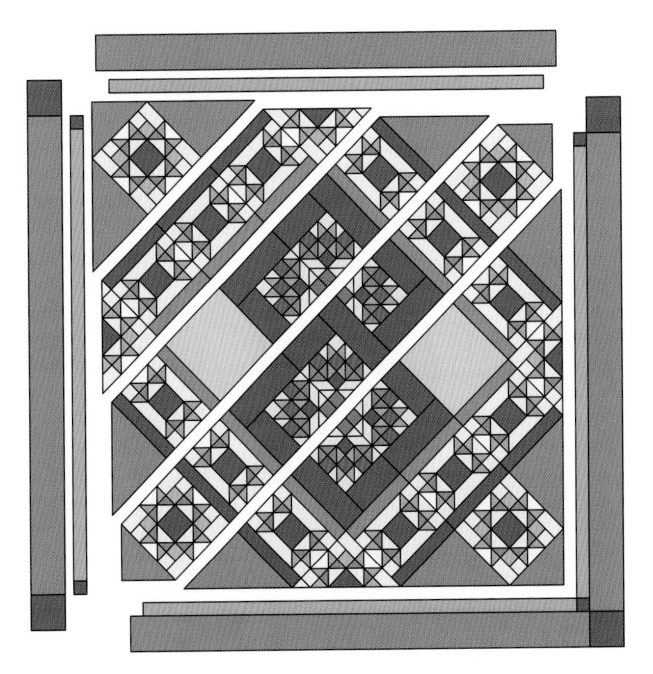

Assembly Diagram

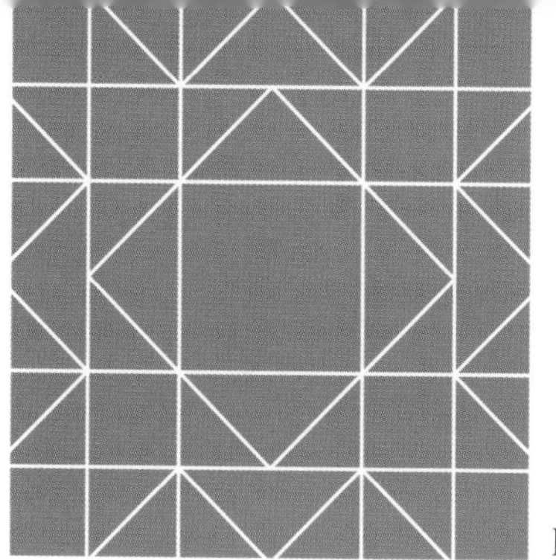

More Design Options

Each of these alternate designs uses an on-point 4 × 4 setting.

8 × 8 grid blocks: B, C1, ½C1, C2, F, L

8 × 8 grid blocks: A, E, F, L, L2

6 × 6 grid blocks: H1, K, ½K, L3, L4, M, X3, X4

6 × 6 grid blocks: A1, I, L4, O, S

8 × 8 grid blocks: B, E1, ½E1 F, L

8 × 8 grid blocks: B, G, L, L2, X2

6 × 6 grid blocks: I, J, K, ½K, L3, M, N1

6 × 6 grid blocks: H1, J, K, ½K, L4, M, X4, ½X4

8 × 8 grid blocks: B, F, L, ¼X2, ½X2

Lavender Sachet

FINISHED SIZE
51″ × 64″

FINISHED BLOCKS
9″

SETTING
On-Point 4 × 5

BLOCKS USED
A1, page 17
H1, page 18
L4, page 23
R, page 26
X4, page 26

Machine quilted by Wanda Jones

For the pretty, feminine look in this quilt, I used background fabric for the corner blocks, which makes the pieced blocks form an oval shape. Careful placement and coloration of the L and X blocks around the perimeter create an appealing border design. The pretty pastel tones enhance the look, while the darker background adds just the right touch of drama.

Materials

See Construction Guidelines, page 74.

tip

Don't get locked into always using white or beige as a background. Color can make a world of difference. Audition different color background fabrics by arranging patches from your quilt blocks on top of a large piece of potential background fabric. Compare a light, medium, and dark in the same color family to see the different moods you can portray with any value, then move on to other colors.

FABRIC	YARDAGE	USED FOR	NUMBER OF PIECES	CUT SIZE
PINK	½ yard	Block A1, piece A	4	2″ × 2″
		Block A1, piece B	12	2″ × 2″
		Block H1, piece A	4	3½″ × 3½″
		Block L4, piece A	10	2″ × 2″
		Block R, piece A	8	3½″ × 3½″
		Block X4, piece A	2	2″ × 2″
BLUE	½ yard	Block A1, piece C	16	2″ × 2″
		Block A1, piece D	8	2⅜″ × 2⅜″
		Block H1, piece B	32	2″ × 2″
		Block H1, piece C	16	2″ × 3½″
YELLOW	¾ yard	Block A1, piece E	4	2″ × 2″
		Block A1, piece G	4	3½″ × 6½″
		Block A1, piece H	4	3½″ × 9½″
		Block H1, piece D	16	2″ × 2″
		Block L4, piece C	40	2″ × 2″
		Block R, piece B	64	2″ × 2″
		Block X4, piece B	8	2″ × 2″
GREEN	½ yard	Block A1, piece F	8	2⅜″ × 2⅜″
		Block H1, piece E	16	2⅜″ × 2⅜″
		Block L4, piece B	20	2″ × 2″
		Block X4, piece C	16	2″ × 2″
LAVENDER	4 yards	Block A1, piece I	8	2″ × 3½″
		Block A1, piece J	8	2⅜″ × 2⅜″
		Block A1, piece K	4	2″ × 2″
		Block H1, piece F	16	2″ × 3½″
		Block H1, piece G	48	2″ × 2″
		Block H1, piece H	16	2⅜″ × 2⅜″
		Block L4, piece D	20	2″ × 2″
		Block L4, piece E	20	2″ × 3½″
		Block L4, piece F	20	2¾″ × 5″
		Block L4, piece G	20	2¾″ × 7¼″
		Block L4, piece H	20	2¾″ × 2¾″
		Block R, piece C	64	2″ × 3½″
		Block R, piece D	32	3½″ × 3½″
		Block X4, piece D	8	2″ × 2″
		Block X4, piece E	8	2¾″ × 5″
		Block X4, piece F	8	2¾″ × 2¾″
		Corner setting blocks	4	9½″ × 9½″

FABRIC	YARDAGE	USED FOR	NUMBER OF PIECES	CUT SIZE
LAVENDER CONTINUED		Setting triangles	4	14¼″ × 14¼″ (Cut twice diagonally for 16 side triangles.)
		Setting triangles	2	7⅜″ × 7⅜″ (Cut once diagonally for 4 corner triangles.)
		Binding	7	2¼″ × fabric width
BACKING	4¼ yards			
BATTING	58″ × 72″			

Construction

Read through these instructions and the Construction Guidelines on page 74 for cutting and piecing techniques before beginning your quilt.

Blocks

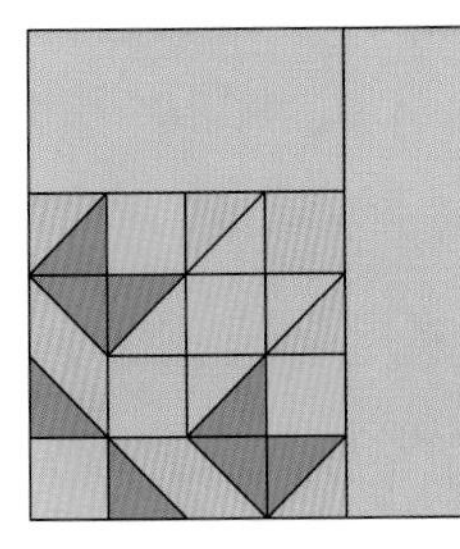

Block A1, make 4 identical. Instructions on page 17.

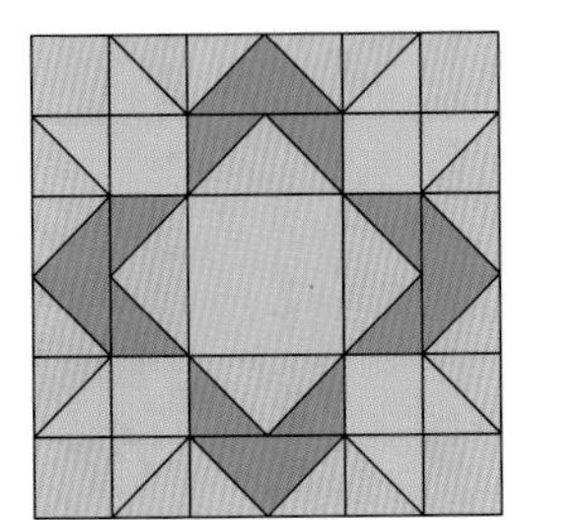

Block H1, make 4 identical. Instructions on page 18.

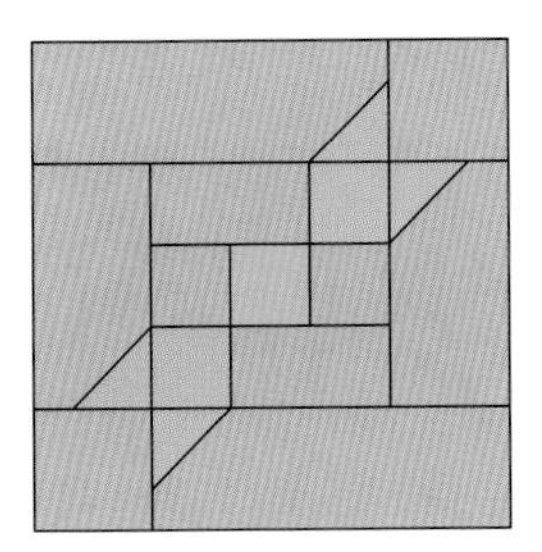

Block L4, make 10 identical. Instructions on page 23.

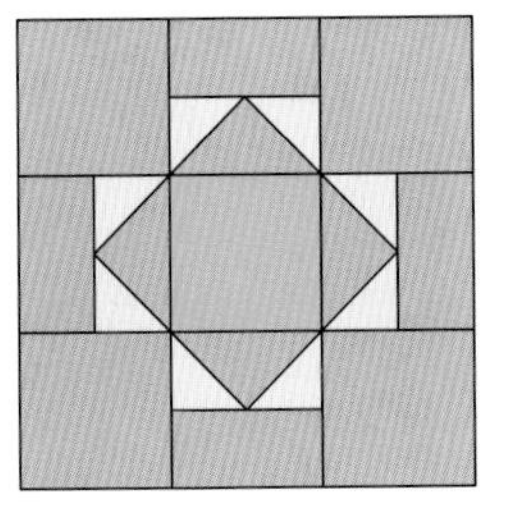

Block R, make 8 identical. Instructions on page 26.

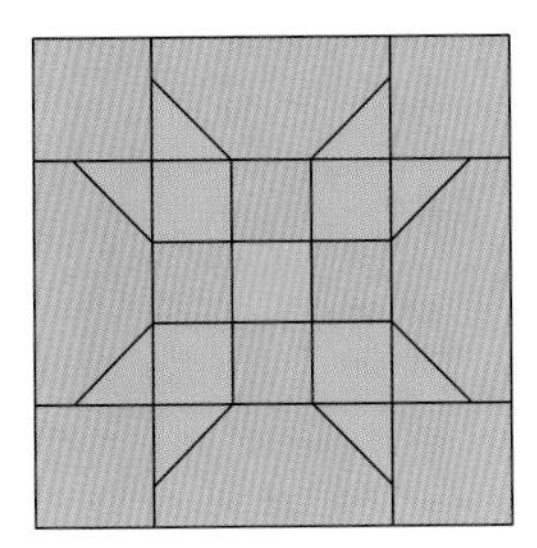

Block X4, make 2 identical. Instructions on page 26.

Refer to the Assembly Diagram to sew the blocks into diagonal rows. Press seams on odd rows to the left and even rows to the right. Sew together rows of blocks to complete the quilt top. Add corner triangles after all rows are sewn together.

Assembly Diagram

Finishing

Prepare the backing (see page 75).

Layer and pin or baste the quilt top, batting, and backing. Quilt as desired.

Prepare the binding (see page 75), and bind the quilt.

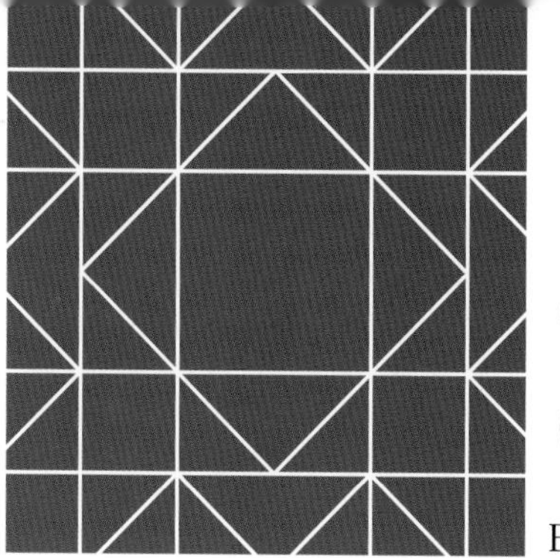

More Design Options

Each of these alternate designs uses an on-point 4 × 5 setting.

6 × 6 grid blocks: A1, H, L4, S, X4

8 × 8 grid blocks: A, B1, C1, G, L

8 × 8 grid blocks: A, B, C1, C2, F, L

8 × 8 grid blocks: B, E1, F, G, L, X1

6 × 6 grid blocks: A1, H1, L4, ½O, O, Q, S, X4

8 × 8 grid blocks: E1, F, G, L, X1

8 × 8 grid blocks: A, B1, C1, F, L

8 × 8 grid blocks: E1, F, G, L, X1

8 × 8 grid blocks: C, C1, E1, L

Ripples in the Stream

Machine quilted by Mary Roder

FINISHED SIZE
75″ × 75″

FINISHED BLOCKS
9″

SETTING
On-Point 5 × 5

BLOCKS USED
A1, page 17
L3, page 22
O, page 25
X4, page 26

This quilt is a real crowd pleaser. The clear colors of the shimmering batiks and the tumbling motion of the A1 blocks give it a watery feel. The gradated values of blue both draw the eye out and pull the quilt together, and the brighter reds appear like water flowers floating on the surface of the quilt. This design is also a good candidate for that secret stash of hand-dyed fabrics you've been saving for a special occasion.

Materials

See Construction Guidelines, page 74.

FABRIC	YARDAGE	USED FOR	NUMBER OF PIECES	CUT SIZE
RED	1¼ yards	Block A1, piece A	25	2″ × 2″
		Block A1, piece C	50	2″ × 2″
		Block A1, piece D	50	2⅜″ × 2⅜″
		Block A1, piece E	25	2″ × 2″
		Block L3, piece C	16	2⅜″ × 2⅜″
		Block O, piece B	16	2″ × 3½″
		Block O, piece D	32	2″ × 2″
		Block X4, piece C	32	2″ × 2″
		First border corner squares	4	2″ × 2″
		Second border corner squares	4	4½″ × 4½″
GREEN	⅝ yard	Block A1, piece B	75	2″ × 2″
		Block L3, piece A	8	3½″ × 3½″
		Block O, piece A	4	3½″ × 3½″
		Block X4, piece A	4	2″ × 2″
MEDIUM BLUE	½ yard	Block A1, piece C	50	2″ × 2″
		Block O, piece C	16	2″ × 2″
LIGHT BLUE	1 yard	Block A1, piece F	50	2⅜″ × 2⅜″
		Block X4, piece B	16	2″ × 2″
		First border	7	2″ × fabric width
DARK BLUE #1	1 yard	Block A1, piece G	13	3½″ × 6½″
		Block A1, piece H	13	3½″ × 9½″
DARK BLUE #2	⅝ yard	Block A1, piece G	6	3½″ × 6½″
		Block A1, piece H	6	3½″ × 9½″
DARK BLUE #3	⅝ yard	Block A1, piece G	6	3½″ × 6½″
		Block A1, piece H	6	3½″ × 9½″
DARK BLUE #4	1¾ yards	Second border	7	4½″ × fabric width
		Binding	8	2¼″ × fabric width
DARK BLUE #5	1 yard	Block L3, piece B	16	2″ × 2″
		Setting triangles	4	14¼″ × 14¼″ (Cut twice diagonally for 16 side triangles.)
		Setting triangles	2	7⅜″ × 7⅜″ (Cut once diagonally for 4 corner triangles.)
ICE BLUE	2¼ yards	Block A1, piece I	50	2″ × 3½″
		Block A1, piece J	50	2⅜″ × 2⅜″
		Block A1, piece K	25	2″ × 2″
		Block L3, piece D	16	2⅜″ × 2⅜″
		Block L3, piece E	16	2″ × 2″

tip

Batik fabrics are undeniably beautiful, but working with these tightly woven fabrics can be a challenge. There are several simple steps you can take to minimize problems. When pinning, use the thinnest, sharpest pins you can find, and use a Microtex rather than a universal needle in your machine. The slender shaft more easily pierces the tight weave. If you are having trouble sewing straight or you hear the needle "punching" through the layers, change needles to keep working with a very sharp point.

FABRIC	YARDAGE	USED FOR	NUMBER OF PIECES	CUT SIZE
ICE BLUE CONTINUED		Block L3, piece F	16	3½″ × 3½″
		Block L3, piece G	16	3½″ × 6½″
		Block O, piece E	48	2″ × 2″
		Block O, piece F	16	2″ × 6½″
		Block X4, piece D	16	2″ × 2″
		Block X4, piece E	16	2¾″ × 5″
		Block X4, piece F	16	2¾″ × 2¾″
BACKING	4½ yards			
BATTING	82″ × 82″			

Construction

Read through these instructions and the Construction Guidelines on page 74 for cutting and piecing techniques before beginning your quilt.

Blocks

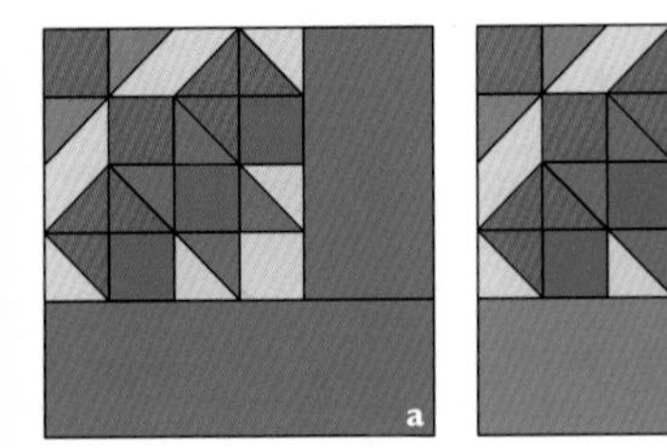

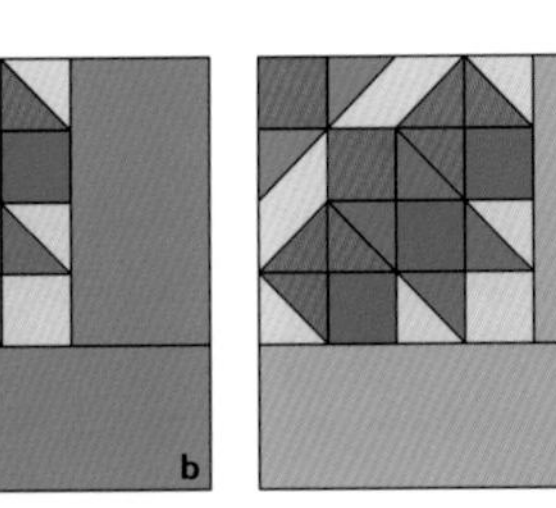

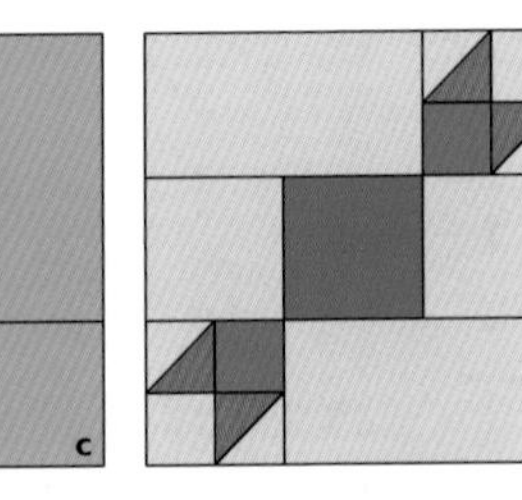

Block A1, make 25 blocks (13 of variation a, 6 each of variations b and c). Instructions on page 17.

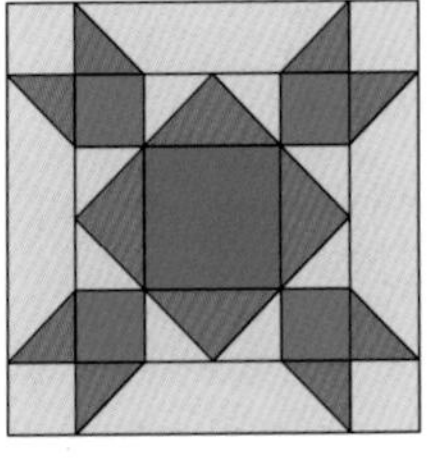

Block L3, make 8 identical. Instructions on page 22.

Block O, make 4 identical. Instructions on page 25.

Block X4, make 4 identical. Instructions on page 26.

Refer to the Assembly Diagram to sew the blocks into diagonal rows. Press seams on odd rows to the left and even rows to the right. Sew together rows of blocks to complete the quilt top. Add corner triangles to row 5 after all rows are sewn together.

Borders

Add the borders one at a time, pressing toward the last border added.

Finishing

Prepare the backing (see page 75).

Layer and pin or baste the quilt top, batting, and backing. Quilt as desired.

Prepare the binding (see page 75), and bind the quilt.

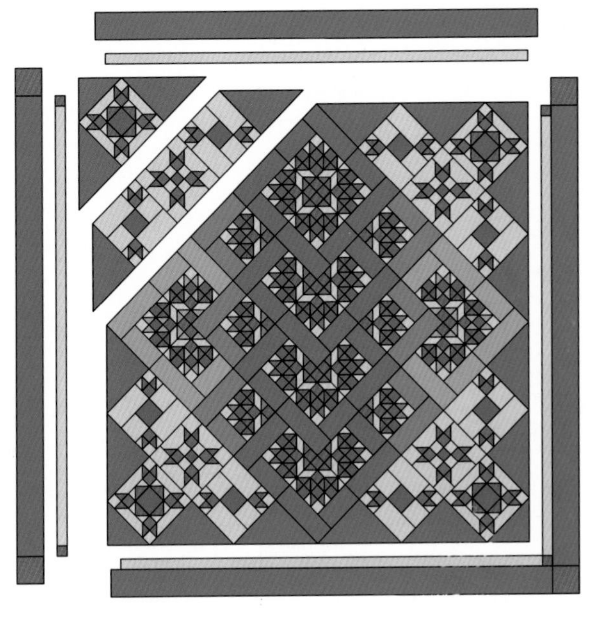

Assembly Diagram

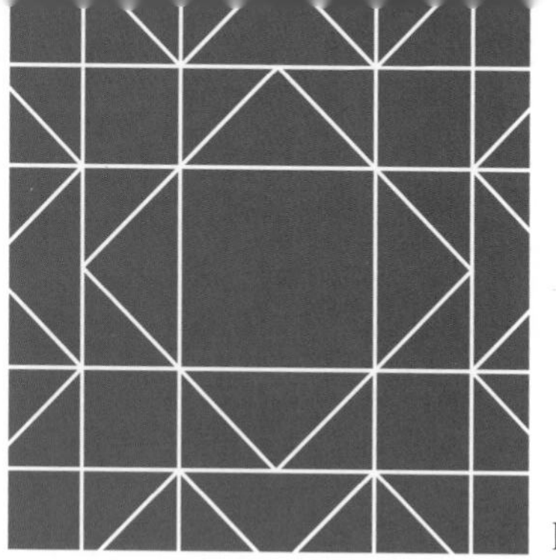

More Design Options

Each of these alternate designs uses an on-point 5 × 5 setting.

6 × 6 grid blocks: H, L3, R, X4

6 × 6 grid blocks: A1, I, L3, X3

8 × 8 grid blocks: A, B1, C, C2, F, G, L

6 × 6 grid blocks: H1, L3, R, X3, X4

8 × 8 grid blocks: A, B1, C1, F, G, L, X

6 × 6 grid blocks: I, L4, N, N1, X3, X4

8 × 8 grid blocks: A, B1, C1, E, F, L, X

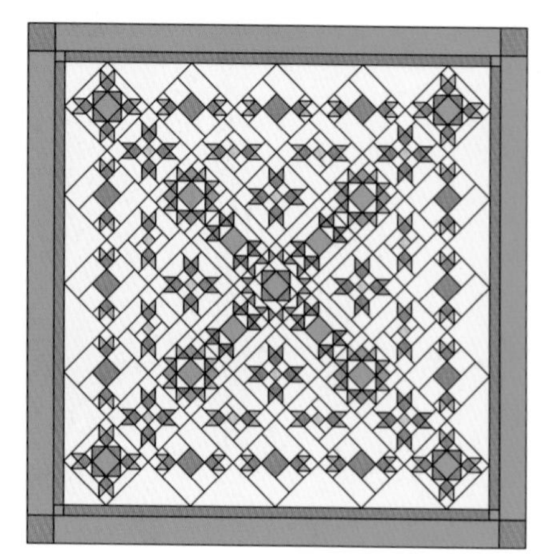

6 × 6 grid blocks: J, K, L3, L4, N1, O, X4

8 × 8 grid blocks: A, B1, F, ½F, ¼F, G, L

Construction Resources

Block Gallery

Here are the Arrow Crown blocks that did not find their way into project quilts in this book. Use these blocks as inspiration for your own creations.

8 x 8 Grid Blocks 1 square = 1½″ ▪ Finished size: 12″

Block B

Block C

Block C2

Block D

Block E

Block L1

Block L2

Block X1

Block X2

6 x 6 Grid Blocks *1 square = 1½″ ▪ Finished size: 9″*

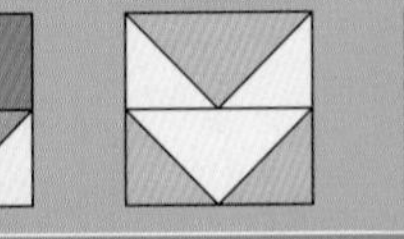

Block H

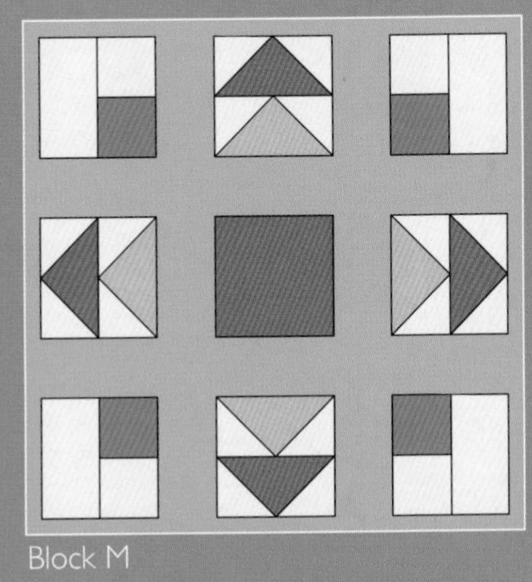

Block M

Block N1

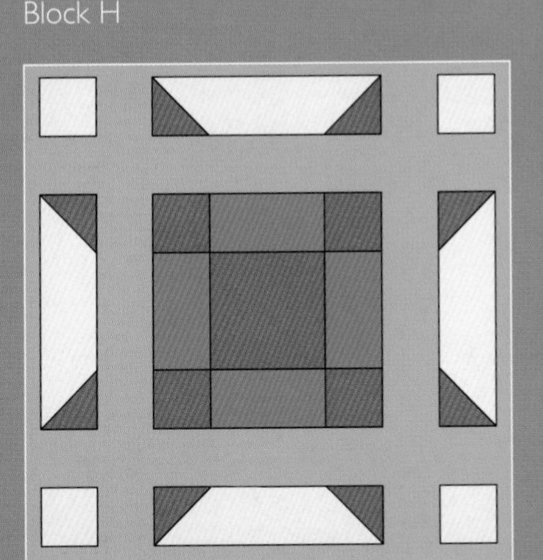

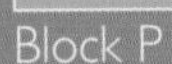

Block P

Block Q

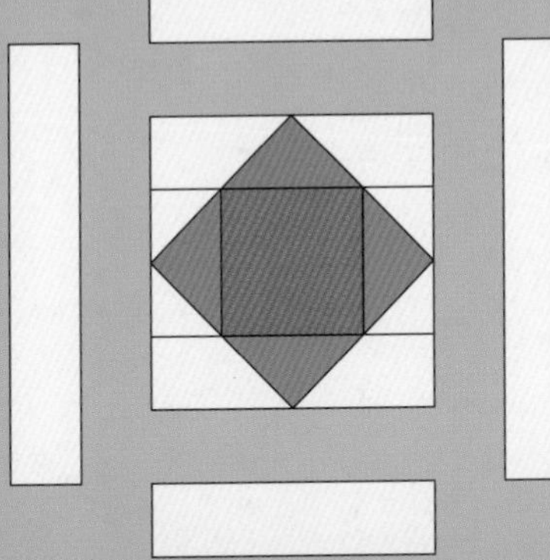

Block S

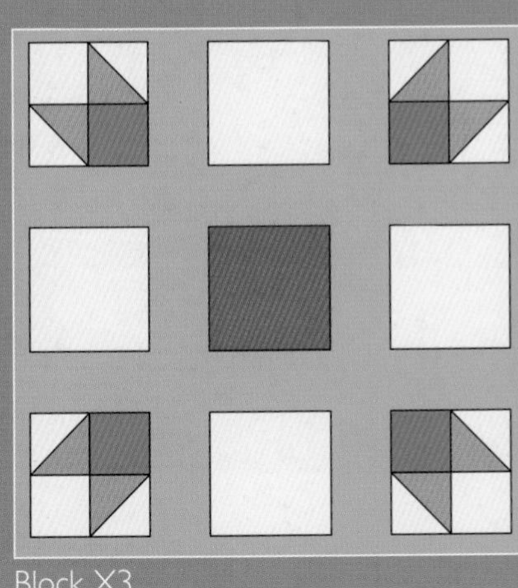

Block X3

Crossover Blocks

Some of the Arrow Crown blocks can work well as both 9″ and 12″ blocks.
To "cross over" an 8 × 8 grid block to a 9″ block, remove the outer rows.

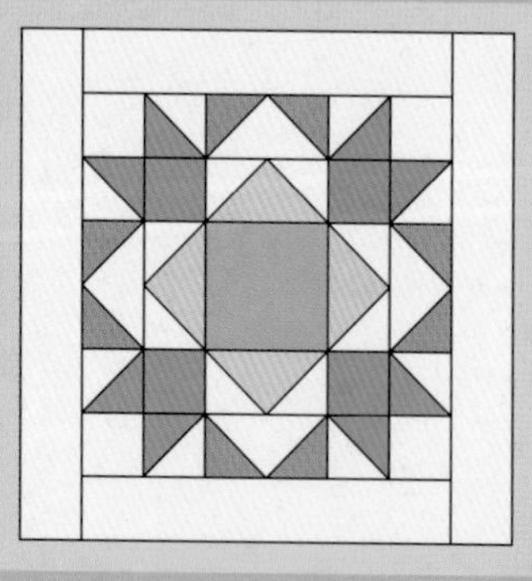

Block D without its outer row is an H block.

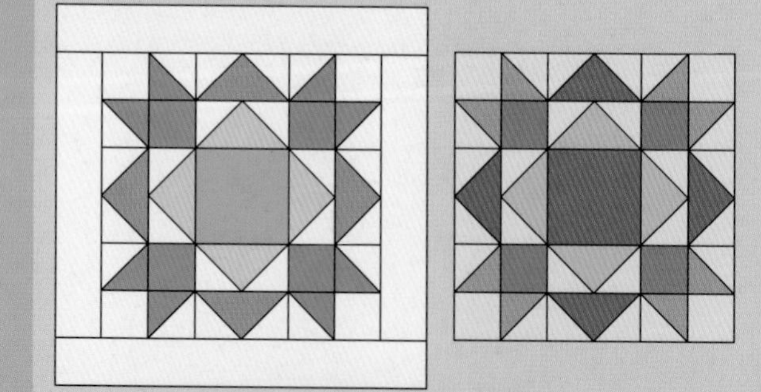

Block E without its outer row is an I block.

Block F without its outer row is an O block.

Block G without its outer row is an N1 block.

To "cross over" a 6 × 6 grid block to a 12″ block, add 1½″ sashing to block: K, M, N, or P.

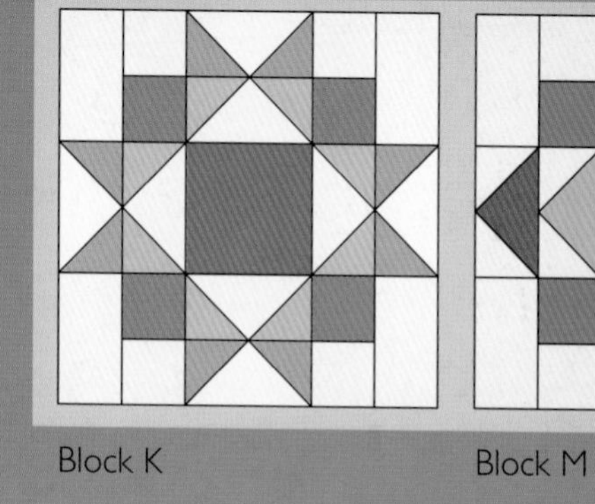

Block K

Block M

Block N

Block P

Gallery

These quilts offer further inspiration on how to use the Arrow Crown block to create unique quilts.

■ *Valentine Wishes*, 54″ × 54″, quilted by Jan Korytkowski

■ *Perfect Pansies*, 48″ × 48″, quilted by Mary Roder

■ *Blended Beauty*, 51″ × 64″, quilted by Jan Korytkowski

■ *Through the Years*, 52″ × 65″, quilted by Jan Korytkowski

Fabric Yardage Chart

BLOCK ________

	color	cut size	# in block	# of blocks	total needed
example	Red	2" x 2"	4	5	20

Use this fill-in-the-blanks chart to quickly and accurately calculate the yardage of each fabric you'll need to complete your quilt. The first line in each chart is an example.

BLOCK ________

	color	cut size	# in block	# of blocks	total needed
example	Blue	2" x 3½"	4	5	20

SETTING TRIANGLES

side triangles

color	# needed	divide by 4	# squares to cut

corner triangles

color	# needed	divide by 2	# squares to cut

NUMBER OF UNITS PER 40" STRIP		
2" x 2"	20	2" strip
2" x 3½"	20	3½" strip
2⅜" x 2⅜"	16	2⅜" strip
2½" x 2½"	16	2½" strip
2¾" x 2¾"	14	2¾" strip
3½" x 3½"	11	3½" strip

The above numbers will help you determine how many strips you need to cut all the pieces required. When cutting longer strips (5", 6½", 9½", 12½"), it is often best to cut a strip that width, and cut the smaller measurement across the width. (For example, to cut 2" x 6½" units, cut a 6½" wide strip, and subcut into 2" pieces.)

STRAIGHT GRAIN STRIPS

sashing

	width x length	# pieces	# strips	strip width	total inches	amt. to buy
ample	2" x 12½"	24	1	12½"		
			2	2"	16½"	⅝ yard

corner blocks

	width x length	# pieces	# strips	strip width	total inches	amt. to buy
ample	2" x 2"	16	1	2"	2"	¼ yard

inner border

width	length	# needed

corner squares

size	# needed

binding

width	length

SUMMARY SHEET

COLOR ___________

size of piece	# of pieces from various blocks	total pieces needed	# of strips to cut	strip width	total inches

Tip

Add $1/4$ to $1/2$ yard to cover bad cuts and changes in design, and for sample blocks. This also gives you extra fabric to piece something interesting on the back of the quilt.

Tip

To cut borders across fabric (selvage to selvage), extra fabric must be allowed for piecing the border strips together at a 45-degree angle. To cut borders on the straight of grain, measure the longest border and buy that length plus $1/4$ yard to allow for variances in piecing and seam allowances. Cut the straight of grain borders before cutting smaller pieces from the yardage.

Construction Guidelines

Read through these basic instructions before making any block or quilt in this book.

Materials

Fabric amounts are based on 42″ of usable fabric width. Borders are cut longer to accommodate actual piecing variances. Borders are cut on the crosswise grain of the fabric and may need to be pieced.

Piecing

All measurements given throughout this book are calculated using a 1/4″ seam allowance.

Sew and Flip Technique

This technique makes triangular patches using only squares and rectangles.

Step 1. Place the two pieces right sides together, aligning the raw edges. Draw a diagonal line from corner to corner of the small square piece.

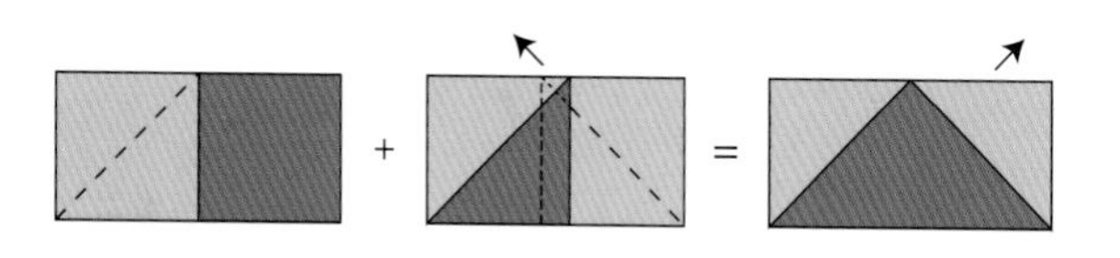

Step 2. Sew along the marked line. Trim the seam allowance to 1/4″, and flip open the top piece; press. Trim the first fabric before you place a second on top of it. Refer to the diagrams for reference as you work.

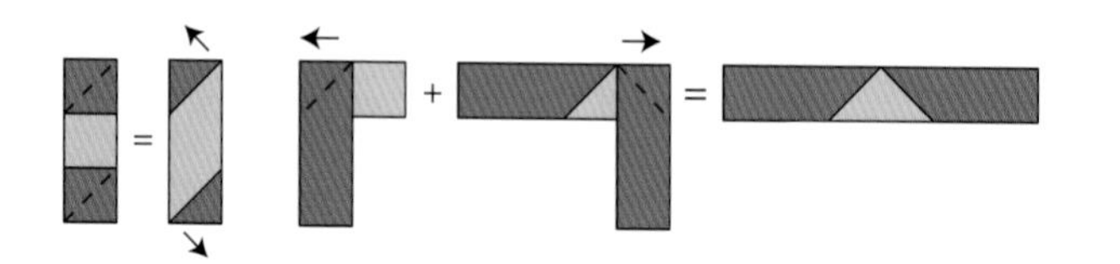

Half-Square Triangles

These units are made from the 2 3/8″ squares listed in the block instructions.

Step 1. Place the two squares right sides together with the lighter color on top, carefully aligning all raw edges. Draw a diagonal line from corner to corner.

Step 2. Sew 1/4″ from the drawn line on each side. Cut the units apart on the drawn line. Press toward the darker triangles.

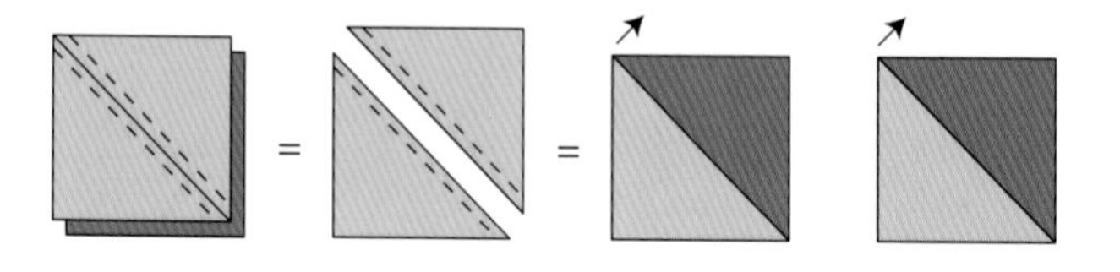

Tip

Half-square triangles can also be made using Triangles on a Roll, or Half Square Triangulations (page 79). Press the units open before removing the papers. The papers stabilize the bias seam and help to prevent stretching out of shape.

Setting Triangles

On-point settings require triangles to fill in the sides and corners once the blocks are set into rows. These are made from squares that are cut diagonally in half (for corner triangles) or in quarters (for side triangles).

Side Triangles

Side triangles are cut from 14¼″ squares for 9″ blocks, or 18¼″ squares for 12″ blocks. Cut each square in half diagonally in both directions; you'll get 4 side triangles from each square. Side triangles are cut slightly larger than needed to allow for individual piecing variances. Once the quilt top is completely pieced, trim the outside edges to a ¼″ seam allowance beyond the block points.

Corner Triangles

Corner triangles are cut from 7⅜″ squares for 9″ blocks, or 9½″ squares for 12″ blocks. These are also cut slightly oversize and will be trimmed when the quilt top is fully assembled. Cut each square in half diagonally in one direction; you'll get 2 corner triangles from each square.

Half and Quarter Blocks

Piece the side and corner setting triangles using full squares on the outside edges, then trim them after piecing. (Be sure to include ¼″ seam allowances.) You cannot simply make a full block and cut it in half or in fourths, because you would have no seam allowance on the cut edge.

Borders

Borders are cut longer than needed to allow for individual piecing differences. Once the quilt top is completely pieced, measure across the width and cut the strips for the first top and bottom border to fit. Sew them to the quilt top, then measure the length of the quilt top and sew these strips to the quilt. Repeat for all additional borders.

If you are adding corner squares in any border, measure all 4 sides of the quilt and cut borders to the same lengths. Sew borders to 2 opposite sides. Sew corner squares to the remaining borders and sew to the quilt. If the quilt is rectangular, the 2 long borders must be equal to each other, and the 2 short borders must be equal to each other.

Tip

If you piece your borders, sew the strips together using diagonal seams. The piecing will be less noticeable.

Diamonds and Triangles

Pieced diamonds and triangles in borders can be tricky to sew exactly. Follow these steps for success. Copy the template pattern, and glue it to template plastic. Cut out the plastic template along the solid line. For ease in matching, punch a small hole where seamlines (dashed lines) meet. Mark a dot on the fabric wrong sides through the punched holes. When piecing and sewing the units together, match these marked dots.

Backing

Yardage for the backing is based on cutting the yardage to the length specified, then piecing the backing with vertical seams. The backing and batting are cut 4″ larger on all sides than the quilt top; this is to allow for piecing differences and an extra "fudge factor."

Binding

Sew the binding strips together using a diagonal seam. The strips are cut for double-fold binding; fold the entire strip in half lengthwise, wrong sides together, and stitch it to the front of the quilt edge. Turn it to the back, and hand sew it with a hidden stitch.

Template Patterns

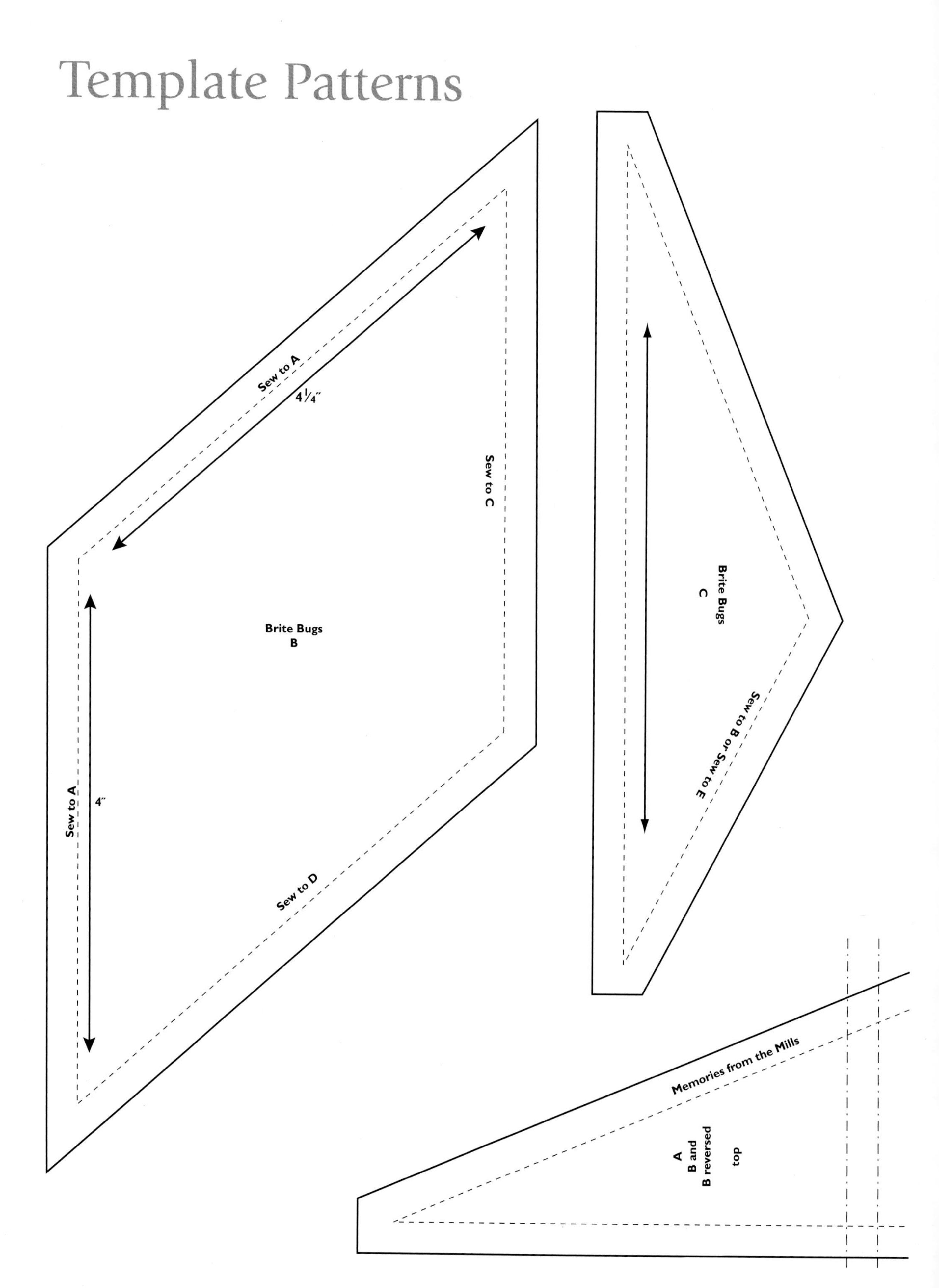

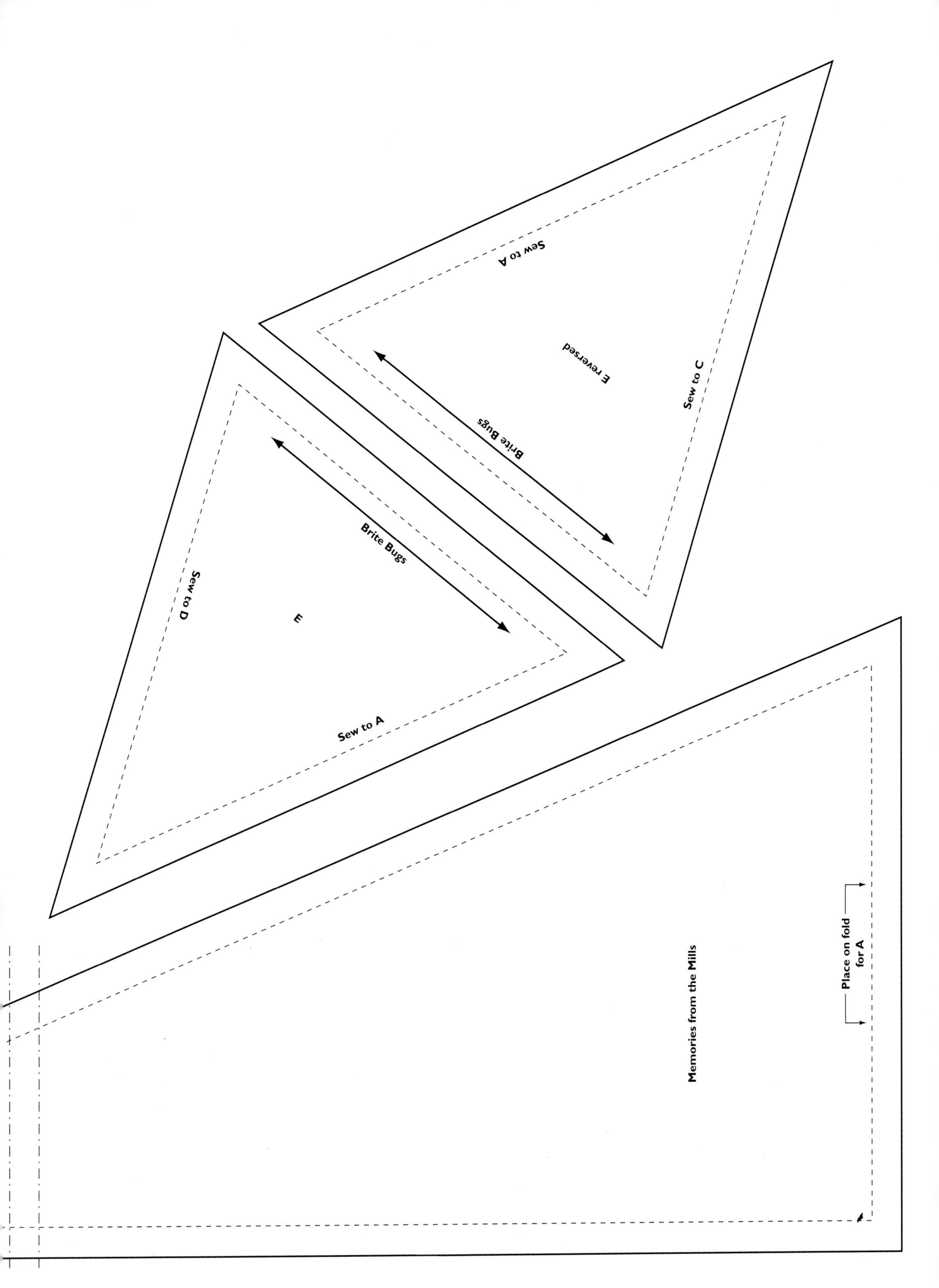
Sew to A
E reversed
Sew to C
Brite Bugs
Brite Bugs
Sew to D
E
Sew to A
Memories from the Mills
Place on fold
for A

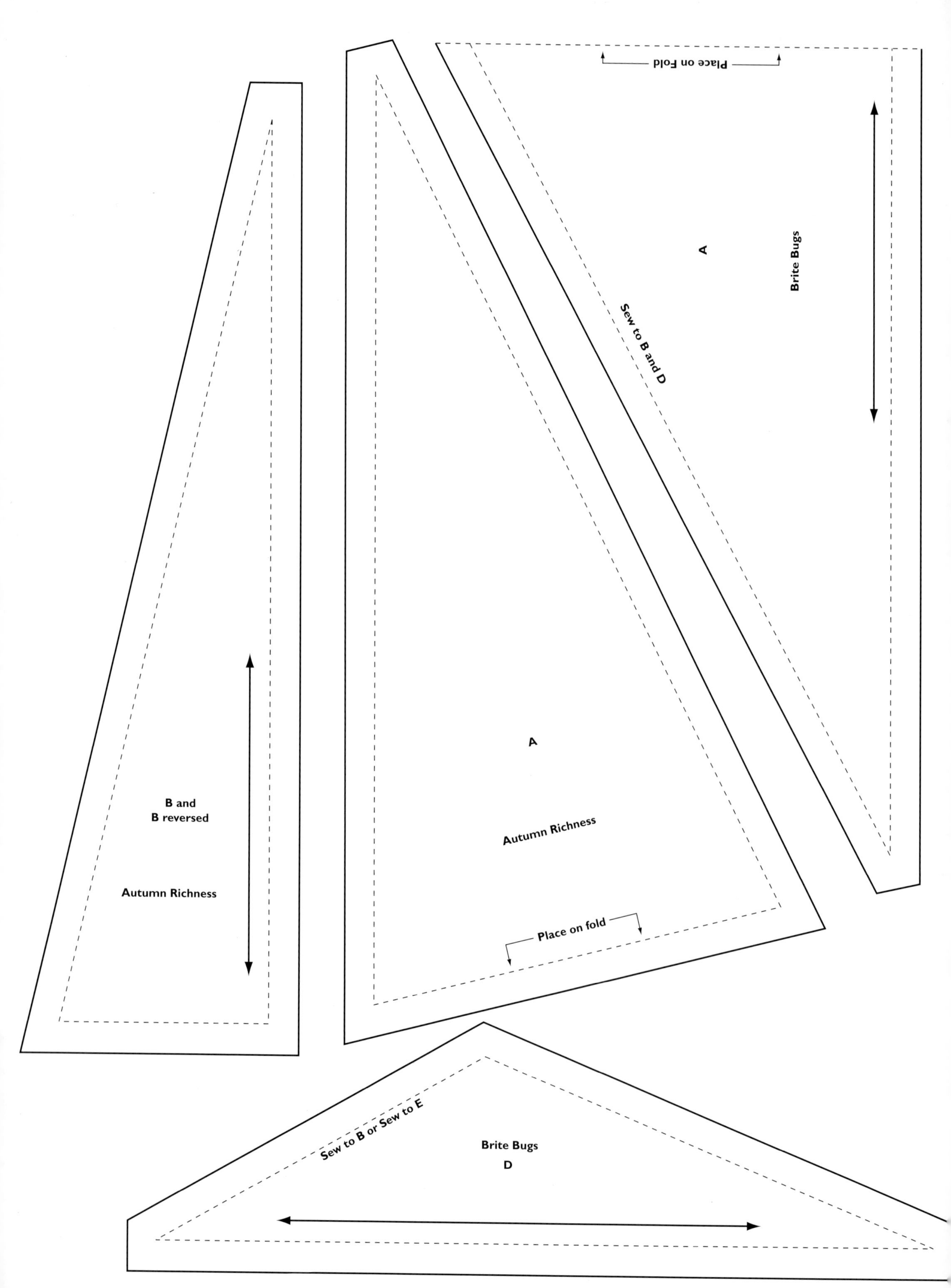
Place on Fold
A
Brite Bugs
Sew to B and D
A
Autumn Richness
Place on fold
B and
B reversed
Autumn Richness
Sew to B or Sew to E
Brite Bugs
D